Feasting on the Living Word of God

Ambassador Of Truth Ministries

Rev. Roger Cole

ISBN 978-1-0980-7048-9 (paperback)
ISBN 978-1-63874-001-8 (hardcover)
ISBN 978-1-0980-7049-6 (digital)

Copyright © 2020 by Rev. Roger Cole

All rights reserved. No part of this publication may be reproduced, distributed, or transmitted in any form or by any means, including photocopying, recording, or other electronic or mechanical methods without the prior written permission of the publisher. For permission requests, solicit the publisher via the address below.

Christian Faith Publishing, Inc.
832 Park Avenue
Meadville, PA 16335
www.christianfaithpublishing.com

Printed in the United States of America

Lesson TLW 1

The Living Word

Dearly beloved, it is my prayer that you and I open our hearts and let God reveal Himself to us in His Word by His Spirit. We will quote some scriptures as we study, and others we will ask you to read. God is a personal God and wants to deal with us individually for our personal spiritual growth. You must never accept everything you read or hear about God's Word unless you can prove it with His Word and have spiritual peace with God about it. Let us pray for wisdom from God and understanding as we feast on the Living Word of God. We can study God's Word for a lifetime and never learn all His truths.

It is our goal in this—the Lord's work—to lift up Jesus in all things so lost souls will be drawn unto Him. Jesus said in John 12:32, "And I, if I be lifted up from the earth, will draw all men unto me."

Read John 8:31–36. If you accept the Truth, Jesus, He shall make you free. That is to say, free from the bondage of sin. Because of the sin of Adam, we are all born sinners (Romans 5:12). That's why Jesus had to make the supreme sacrifice for all the sins of the world with His sinless blood (Romans 5:6–11).

Jesus said in John 14:6, "I am the Way, the Truth, and the Life; no man cometh unto the Father, but my me." He has the right to claim that, for He is the One that died for you and me, not any other person. Acts 4:12 says, "Neither is there salvation in any other: for there is none other name under heaven given among men, whereby we must be saved."

In the book of John chapter 1, there is much revealed to us. We will look at a few verses. Verses 1 to 3 says, "In the beginning was the Word, and the Word was with God, and the Word was God. The same was in the beginning with God. All things were made by him; and without him was not anything made that was made." We must understand that God had no beginning. He has always existed. Man had a beginning from God the Creator. Thus, this is when time as we know it began for man.

Using verse 14 of John chapter 1, we can conclude that the Word is Jesus Christ. Thus, Jesus is the Living Word. He was with God, and He is God. This may be hard for you to understand. Fear not, God is not the author of confusion (1 Corinthians 14:33).

In John chapter 17, we find Jesus praying to His Father. Read this chapter carefully. You will learn much. Look at verse 5: "And now, O Father, glorify thou me with thine own self with the glory which I had with Thee before the world was." As you see, Jesus was talking about His existing before the world was.

In Genesis 1:26, we see "And God said Let us make man in our image, after our likeness." *Us* refers to the Godhead, which is the Father, the Son, and the Holy Spirit.

Jesus came to earth from heaven to be born of a virgin (Mary), to live a sinless life in a human body with complete obedience to the Heavenly Father, to die a cruel death on the cross of Calvary for your sins and mine, and to *rise again*, conquering death and the grave so we may have that *blessed hope of eternal life* in Him. Jesus rose from the grave and lives forever more. Jesus *is* the Living Word.

May God richly bless you as you study His Word.

Yours in Christ,

Rev. Roger D. Cole

Lesson TLW 2

Jesus Christ, God in the Flesh

Was Jesus God in the flesh? The answer is yes. Jesus was God, the Son, in the flesh. As we see in John 1:1 and 14, Jesus is referred to as God. In Isaiah 7:14, there is a prophesy of a virgin that would conceive and bear a son and shall call his name Immanuel. Matthew 1:23 tells us the same and explains that Immanuel means "God with us." The angel of the Lord appeared to Joseph and explained how and why Mary was with child, and the child shall be called Jesus. Since the child was to be called Immanuel, meaning "God with us," and also was told to give the child the name Jesus, we can conclude that the names can be interchanged. Jesus was God in the flesh. Yet Jesus is the Savior of the world. God took upon Himself to come down to earth in the form of man, leaving all His Glory for a time so that He could make the supreme sacrifice that could be sufficient payment for the sins of the world.

Mary was truly blessed of God to be chosen the virgin that would conceive and bring forth the Christ child, Jesus, Immanuel, the Savior of the world. In Luke chapter 1, we see that Elisabeth, the cousin of Mary, referred to the unborn child of Mary as her Lord. Mary said these words in verse 46 and 47 of Luke chapter 1, "And Mary said, My soul doth magnify the Lord, and my spirit hath rejoiced in God my Savior." This woman, Mary, who found favor with God, realized who was living in her body. She referred to the child as Lord and God and Savior. You must understand, even though

Mary was chosen of God for this task, Mary was born a sinner, just like you and I were, because of Adam. Consequently, she realized she had need of a Savior to save her soul from eternal damnation. She called Jesus Lord, which means "Supreme in authority or controller" of her life. The person of Mary, the living soul, magnified the Lord. Her spirit, the innermost part of her (the mind and heart) rejoiced in God, her Savior. Thus, we must conclude from what Mary said that Jesus was God in the flesh, Immanuel, and He was her Savior and Lord of her life. Mary had a wonderful relationship with God. How is your relationship with God? Have you accepted Jesus as your Savior? Have you made Jesus Lord (Ruler) over your life? You must realize who Jesus is for you to have that blessed hope of eternal life.

In John 20:28, Apostle Thomas called Jesus Lord and God: "And Thomas answered and said unto Him, my Lord and my God." In chapter 1 of Hebrews, we see God calling the Son God (verse 8). Jesus received worship in Matthew 14:33. Only God is to be worshipped. Angels refused worship in Revelation 22:8 and 9. Man refused worship (Acts 10:25, 26). Jesus forgives sin (Mark 2:5–11). Only God can forgive sin. Jesus has all power in heaven and in earth (Matthew 28:18). Jesus controls the universe He created (Hebrews 1:3), and without Him, you and I can do nothing (John 15:5). Jesus did many mighty works while on earth. To write all the wonderful works He has done in books, the world could not hold them.

My friend, do you know Jesus, who was God in the flesh? Have you allowed Him to control your life? Do you live for Him who died for you? Do you have peace with God? Do you have joy in your heart? If you died today, do you know your eternal destiny? Is it *heaven* or *hell*? Don't forget John 3:16 and John 14:6.

Yours in Christ,

Ambassador of Truth Ministries A3

The Study of the Word of God

Introduction

Why should anyone study the Word of God? Your reason may differ from others. But this is quite common. Some want to learn about creation. Some want to learn about the nation of Israel. Some want to learn about prophesy. Some want to learn about God. Some want to learn about Satan. Some want to learn about Jesus.

Whatever reason you may have at first will not matter, as you grow in knowledge and wisdom in the Word of God. As you come closer to the *Truth* (Jesus), you will want to study so you may have a closer walk with Him. Second Timothy 2:15 says, "Study to show thyself approved unto God, a workman that needeth not to be ashamed, rightly dividing *the word of truth.*"

In studying the word of *God*, you will learn many things that will help you live the life God wants you to live. By learning God's Word and applying it to your life, you will have power to overcome Satan. You must understand that Satan is the prince and power of the air. You and I can never defeat Satan on our own. We must do as Jesus did with Satan and use the Word of God to overcome any temptation.

At first, things that are said may be strange to you. Have no fear; God's Word is Truth. God is not the author of confusion. You must realize that God will show what He knows you need at your stage of life if you are truly a Christian.

What is a Christian? Some say I was born a Christian. Others may say that they belong to this church or that church. Then some may say I am a good person; therefore, I am a Christian.

The word *Christian* means to be Christlike. In other words, a Christian is to live his or her life like Christ would live it. Please remember, Jesus is the same yesterday, today, and forever. In John 14:6, Jesus said, "I am *the Way, the Truth, and the Life: no man cometh to the Father, but by me.*"

As you see, Jesus is the only way to heaven or to the Heavenly Father. Should you die this moment, do you know for sure that you will go to heaven? If you have any doubts, do not hesitate to find out how you can know.

Since we know that Jesus is the *truth*, we must accept what He says we must do to go to heaven. In John 3:3, Jesus said, "Verily, verily, I say unto thee, Except a man be born again, he cannot see the Kingdom of God." Jesus goes on to explain what this means in verses 5 and 6. To go to heaven, we must be born of the flesh and then be born of the Spirit. Everyone is born with a soul. The destination of this soul is determine by each individual person. We must *all* give an account to God. Because of Adam's sin, we are all born sinners, and we are doomed for eternal hell without Christ as our Lord and Savior. His blood was shed for our sins.

John 3:16 says, "For God so loved the world, that he gave his only begotten Son, that whosoever believeth in him should not perish but have everlasting life." Jesus said in John 12:32, "And I, if I be lifted up from the earth, will draw all men unto me." Jesus was talking about how His dying upon the cross of Calvary would draw all men unto Him. He is telling us that sometime in one's life, he or she will have an opportunity to come unto Him for salvation of their soul. *You* cannot come to Jesus for salvation at your convenience. Jesus said in John 6:44, "No man can come to me, except the Father which hath sent me draw him: and I will raise him up at the last day."

The Holy Spirit of God will urge your heart to repent of your sins, believe the gospel, and accept Jesus Christ as your Lord and

Savior. The Holy Spirit will draw you unto Jesus as you hear the Word of God. Then by faith, you will receive Jesus into your heart. Romans 10:17 says, "So then faith cometh by hearing, and hearting by the Word of God."

When you repent and receive Jesus into your heart, at that moment, Jesus comes and lives in your heart through the Holy Spirit of God. At that moment, you become a tabernacle of God, for God lives in you through His Spirit.

Upon salvation, you have experienced the new birth. In other words, you are born again. This means that your soul is saved from eternal damnation. This also means that your soul is sealed until the day of redemption. When Jesus said that you have everlasting life, it means forever and forever, through eternity.

You are born again. Thus, your life should be changed. Second Corinthians 5:17 says, "Therefore if any man be in Christ, he is a new creature: old things are passed away; behold all things are become new." If you go to places that do not glorify God, and you still do things that Jesus would not do, then you better repent and accept Jesus. For one continuing in sin shows that he or she does not know God. Do you love God? Prove it. Serve Him and be blessed.

When you come to understand the true meaning of salvation of your soul through the new birth, then you will want to learn how this new creature should live. You can only know through the study of the Word of God. Be not afraid. Holy men of God wrote the words of the Bible as they were moved by the Holy Spirit of God. Second Peter 1:20–21 says, "Knowing this first, that no prophecy came not in old time by the will of man: but holy men of God spake as they were moved by the Holy Ghost." Consequently, upon your new birth, the Holy Spirit of God comes and lives in you; He will teach you all things of Christ through His Word. He will show, through His Word, the things that you need each day to glorify your Heavenly Father.

God will give you the strength to overcome Satan. He will give you grace to overcome any obstacles that may come before you. He will give you the peace that pass all understanding. The Holy Spirit will convict you of sin in your life, and at that moment, you as a child of God must repent and ask God for forgiveness if you want to be in fellowship of God.

As long as we have this fleshy body, we will sin; even as a Christian. Always remember this, God does *not* fellowship with sin. In writing to Christians in 1 John, we see in the first chapter verses 8–10, "If we say that we have no sin, we deceive ourselves, and the *truth* is not in us. If we confess our sins, he is faithful and just to forgive us our sins, and to cleanse us from all unrighteousness. If we say that we have not sinned, we make him a liar, and his word is not in us."

First John 2:1–6, says, "My little children, these things write I unto you, that ye sin not. And if any man sin, we have an advocate with the Father, Jesus Christ the righteous; And he is the propitiation for our sins; and not for ours only, but also for the sins of the whole world. And hereby we do know that we know him, if we keep his commandments. He that saith, I know him, and keepeth not his commandments, is a liar and the *truth* is not in him. But whoso keepeth his word, in him verily is the love of God perfected: hereby know we that we are in him. He that saith he abideth in him ought himself also so to walk, even as he walked."

Please remember, you and I cannot do this on our own. God has given us His only begotten Son to die the sin death in your place and mine. He has given us His Word as a roadmap to heaven. In other words, He shows us how we should live to please Him while we are here on this earth. God has given us, upon our new birth, the Holy Spirit of God to teach us through His Word. After learning truth from the Word of God, the Holy Spirit leads us in our daily lives to use these truths for the glory of God.

Ambassador of Truth Ministry

The Study of the Word of God

In the Old Testament of the Word of God, in the book of Deuteronomy 29:29, we see these words: "The secret things belong unto the Lord our God: but those things which are revealed belong unto us and to our children forever, that we may do all the words of this law.

We are God's creation, made in His image. Adam and Eve were exactly that. They were made in the image of God. They were without sin upon creation. However, God made them with a will. This will was to give them a choice, either to serve Him and receive the blessings or disobey His will and reap the penalty. After yielding to temptation by Satan, Adam and Eve sinned against God. Because of their sin, they were cast out of the garden of Eden. They did not realize the shame of their nakedness until they sinned. Thus, God shed the blood of animals and took the skins and covered their nakedness. This was a lesson to teach Adam and Eve—that without the shedding of blood, there is no remission for sin.

Because of Adam's sin, all humanity are born sinners. Therefore, all—I said, *all*—must have their sins covered by the blood. This blood is the blood that was shed on the cross of Calvary for you and me by our Lord and SAVIOR Jesus Christ, the only begotten Son of God (John 3:16). Jesus is on the right hand of the Heavenly Father, making intercession for all Christians when they pray to the Heavenly Father in Jesus's name. Jesus shed His blood for our sins.

No one else has the right to go to the Heavenly Father to make intercession for us. No one else can save you.

In the book of Acts chapter 4, we see Apostle Peter speaking to the high priest. Verses 8–12 says, "Then Peter, filled with the Holy Ghost, said unto them, Ye rulers of the people, and elders of Israel, If this day be examined of the good deed done to the impotent man, by what means he is made whole; Be it known unto you all, and to all the people of Israel, that by the name of Jesus Christ of Nazareth, whom ye crucified, whom God raised from the dead, even by him doth this man stand here before you whole. This is the stone which was set at nought of you builders, which is become the head of the corner. Neither is there salvation in any other: for there is none other name under heaven given among men, whereby we must be saved."

Jesus was from the beginning and is everlasting. The main purpose of the Word of God is to point us to Christ for the salvation of our souls so we can then fellowship with our Heavenly Father with peace and joy in our souls.

Throughout the ages, Satan has tried to destroy the Word of God. Many times, people were forced to burn all their Bibles. However, the Word of God is still here today. Satan saw that it would be impossible to get everyone to burn their Bibles. Therefore, he devised a sly way to try to destroy the power of the Word of God. He got man to start making different translations. Consequently, he knew words would be added and some taken away from the Word of God. You can read some easy-to-read Bibles today, but you will get the blessings you deserve by reading the Word of God.

Satan has raised up many wolves in sheep's clothing throughout the ages to deliver a false message so that many, many souls will not come to Jesus for true salvation. Some religions lead people to think that they can work their way to heaven. Jesus is the only way.

Second Peter 2:1–2 says, "But there were false prophets also among the people, even as there shall be false teachers among you, who privily shall bring in damnable heresies, even denying the Lord that bought them, and bring upon themselves swift destruction. And many shall follow their pernicious ways; by reason of whom the way of truth shall be evil spoken of."

For every good thing God has to offer, Satan has a copy, which seems to be the same but isn't. In chapter 11 of the book of 2 Corinthians, Apostle Paul tells the church at Corinth to beware of false preachers and teachers. Let's look at verses 1–15: "Would to God ye could bear with me a little in my folly: and indeed bear with me. For I am jealous over you with godly jealousy: for I have espoused you to one husband, that I may present you as a chaste virgin to Christ. But I fear, least by any means, as the serpent beguiled Eve through his subtilty, so your minds should be corrupted from the *simplicity* that is in Christ. For he that cometh preacheth another Jesus, whom we have not preached, or if ye receive another spirit, which we have not received, or another gospel, which ye have not accepted, ye might well bear with him. For I suppose I was not a whit behind very chiefest apostle. But though I be rude in speech, yet not in knowledge; but we have been thoroughly made manifest among you in all things. Have I committed an offense in abasing myself that ye might be exalted, because I have preached to you the gospel of God freely? I robbed other churches, taking wages of them, to do your service. And when I was present with you, and wanted, I was chargeable to no man: for that which was lacking to me the brethen which came from Macedonia supplied: and in all things I have kept myself from being burdensome unto you, and so will I keep myself. As the truth of Christ is in me, no man shall stop me of this boasting in the regions of Achaia. Wherefore? Because I love you not? God knoweth. But what I do that I will do, that I may cut off occasion from them which desire occasion; that wherein they glory, they may be found even as we. For such are false apostles, deceitful workers, transforming themselves into the apostles of Christ. And no marvel; for Satan himself is transformed into an angel of light. Therefore it is no great thing if his ministers also be transformed as the ministries of righteousness; whose end shall be according to their works." (italics mine)

In the study of the Word of God, you will find that God repeats many of the same teachings. We will teach in the same matter so you and I will learn them more.

Rev. Roger D. Cole

Ambassador of the Truth Ministry A2

The Study of the Word of God

Origin of KJV

The Word of God is the same yesterday, today, and forever. The original manuscripts were handed down many generations. These manuscripts were written by man through the moving of the Holy Spirit of God. Second Peter 1:20–21 says, "Knowing this first, that no prophecy of the scripture is of any private interpretation. For the prophecy came not in old time by the will of man: but holy men of God spake as they were moved by the Holy Ghost."

With age, the original manuscripts started to decay. Therefore, copies of the original manuscripts had to be made to preserve the Word of God. These were copies exactly like they were in the original languages written.

As the Word of God spread into other parts of the world, the English-speaking people wanted to have the Word of God in their language. Other countries felt the same way. Therefore, there was a need to translate the original manuscripts into other languages.

We know that the original manuscripts were written in the Arabic, the Hebrew, the Chaldee, and the Greek languages. The English-speaking people wanted to have the Word of God translated into their language. Thus, there were some scholars who did so, even though most of these were incomplete. The most important English-version Bible ever to be produced is sometimes called the Authorized Version and sometimes the King James Version. In the summer of 1603, when King James was on his way to London to receive the English crown, he was presented with a petition of grievances by the clergy of Puritan convictions, which led the king to call a conference "for hearing and for the determining of things pretended to be amiss in the church." This conference was convened three days, January 14–16, 1604, and known as the Hampton Court Conference. During this conference, Dr. John Reynolds, the leader of the Puritan party and president of Corpus Christi College, Oxford, made the motion that a new translation of the Bible be undertaken. Fifty-four of the greatest biblical scholars in Great Britain were brought together for this great task, divided into six groups—three to work on a translation of the Old Testament and three on the New Testament. The Translation was to be done from the original manuscripts.

There being a lapse of two or three years between the naming of these committees and the beginning of their labors, the work was begun in 1607 and completed in 1610. The Bible appeared in the year 1611 as the Authorized Version for the English-speaking people (KJV).

Many people, throughout the ages, have tried to discredit the Word of God. The first one to try this was the father of all lies, Satan. In the book of Genesis chapter 3, we see how Satan quotes the Word of God correctly. However, we see how Satan interprets God's Word to be satisfying to the flesh of man. God had created Adam and Eve in a perfect sinless state in the image of God.

God gave them a will (a mind to decide for themselves), whether to obey God and live or disobey and die. If Adam and Eve had obeyed God, they would not have died spiritually or physically. Because of their sin, their souls were doomed for hell. But God's infinite mercy saw fit to have someone else die the sin death in their place. God killed an animal and took the skin to cover their nakedness (Genesis 3:21). Hebrews chapter 9 explains the purpose of the shedding of blood, both in the Old Covenant and the New Covenant. Jesus Christ not only died the sin death for Adam and Eve, but He died the sin death for *all humanity*. This includes you and me. John 3:16 says, "For God so loved the world, that he gave his only begotten Son, that whosoever believeth in him should not perish, but have everlasting life." Due to the fall of Adam and Eve, all men and women are born of the flesh: sinners. Thus, only a sacrifice of sinless blood could pay the penalty of sin.

Satan has always tried to keep people from knowing the truth, which he knows will set them free from the bondage of sin. That is why he has conceived many different ways to deceive us.

Satan had to resort to his original method. That method is to have men to interpret the Word of God to almost perfection, changing a little here and there. This method has been very successful. However, this is very deadly. Revelation 22:18–19 says, "For I testify unto every man that heareth the words of the prophecy of this book, If any man shall add unto these things, God shall add unto him the plagues that are written in this book: And if any shall take away from the words of the book of this prophecy, God shall take away his part of the book of life, and out of the holy city, and from the things which are written in this book."

You may start to understand why it is best to stay with the Word of God that has stood all the tests throughout history: the King James Version.

Satan has brought many of his followers through the ages to mislead people in the Word of God. He could not destroy the Word. That is why he has encouraged people to make many different translations of the Word of God. Satan knows the more you will translate the Word, the more people will add or take away from the truth. In doing this, Satan knows that many will follow him instead of follow Jesus.

We are here to proclaim the truth. What you do with the truth, Jesus, is up to you. I cannot force you to get saved or force you to serve God after salvation. These important decisions are for you and you alone to decide. It is your soul you must answer for. Heaven or hell—the choice is yours. Don't let Satan hold you back from doing what God wants you to do. God loves you, not Satan.

REV. ROGER COLE

May God richly bless you as you yield to God's will for your life. You have not really lived until you start living for Jesus.

Yours in Christ Jesus,
Brother R. D.

Rev. Roger D. Cole

Ambassador of Truth Ministries A1

The Way to Heaven

Every one of us would like to go to heaven. However, many of us do not fully understand what we must do to go to heaven. There are some that say we must belong to this church or that church in order to go to heaven. Some may say we must do this or that in order to go to heaven. My friend, there are many things that we do not seem to understand. But we can know the right way if we believe the Word of God. The Word of God is our road map to heaven. You must follow its direction if you want to reach that destination. You must not believe what man tells you if it does not agree with the Word of God. We are talking about your soul, which is eternal. Which means that your soul will either be in heaven or hell forever after you die. This is a serious business concerning your soul. It is my prayer to read this lesson in order for you to be sure about where your soul is going after death. God loves you and wants you to go to be with Him in heaven. But He allows you the choice. Through His Word, He shows you how you can get to heaven. In this lesson, we will try to help you.

    The Word of God is the same today, yesterday, and forever. The original manuscripts were handed down through many generations. Those manuscripts were written by man through the moving of the Holy Spirit of God. Second Peter 1:20–21 says, "Knowing this first, that no prophecy of the scripture is of any private interpretation. For the prophecy came not in old time by the will of man: but holy men of *God* spake as they were moved by the *Holy Ghost*."

Many people throughout the ages have tried to discredit the Word of God. The first one to try this was the father of all lies, Satan himself. In the book of Genesis chapter 3, we see how Satan quotes the Word of God correctly. However, we see how Satan interpret God's Word to be satisfying to the flesh of man. God had created Adam and Eve in a perfect sinless state, in the image of God.

God gave them a will (a mind to decide for themselves), whether to obey God and live or disobey and die. If Adam and Eve had obeyed God, they would not have died spiritually or physically. Because of their sin, their souls were doomed for hell. But God's infinite mercy saw fit to have someone else die the sin death in their place. God killed an animal and took the skin to cover their nakedness (Genesis 3:21). Hebrews chapter 9 explains the purpose of the shedding of blood, both in the Old Covenant and the New Covenant. Jesus Christ not only died the sin death for Adam and Eve, but He died the sin death for all sinners. This includes you and me. John 3:16 says, "For God so loved the world, that he gave his only begotten Son, that whosoever believeth in him should not perish, but have everlasting life." Due to the fall of Adam and Eve, all men and women are born of the flesh: sinners. Thus, only a sacrifice of sinless blood could pay the penalty of sin.

Jesus Christ was born of a virgin, Mary. This was prophesied in the Old Testament in the book of Isaiah 7:14, which says, "Therefore the Lord himself shall give you a sign; Behold, a virgin shall conceive, and bear a son, and shall call his name Immanuel." The Jews were always looking for signs. There are many people today that look for signs. However, it seems that they are just as the Jews were in the time of Christ; they reject Him and follow commandments of men instead of God.

Mary was blessed of God in having the privilege of being the *earthly* mother of the Christ-child. You must understand that Jesus Christ was in existence before the creation of the world. In Genesis 1:26, God said, "Let *us* make man in *our* image, after our likeness." *Us* and *our* are in reference to the Father, the Son, and the Holy

Ghost; for they are *one*. Ephesians 3:9–12 says, "And to make all men see what is the fellowship of the mystery, which from the beginning of the world hath been hid in God, who created all things by Jesus Christ: To the intent that now unto the principalities and powers in heavenly places might be known by the church the manifold wisdom of God, According to the eternal purpose which he purposed in Christ Jesus our Lord: In whom we have boldness and access with confidence by the faith of him." There are many scriptures that show us that Christ was in existence before creation.

Let us look at the Gospel according to Apostle John. Chapter 1:1–14 says,

> In the beginning was the Word, and the Word was with God, and the Word was God. The same was in the beginning with God. All things were made by him; and without him was not any thing made that was made. In him was life; and life was the light of men. And the light shineth in darkness; and the darkness comprehended it not. There was a man sent from God, whose name was John. The same came for a witness, to bear witness of the Light., that all men through him might believe. He was not that Light, but was sent to bear witness of that Light. That was the true Light, which lighteth every man that cometh into the world. He was in the world, and the world was made by him, and the world knew him not. He came unto his own, and his own received him not. But as many as received him, to them gave him power to become the sons of God, even to them that believe on his name: Which were born, not of blood, nor of the will of the flesh, nor of the will of man, but of God. And the word was made flesh, and dwelt among us (*and we beheld his glory, the glory as of the only begotten of the Father,*) full of grace and truth.

Verse 14 tells us that the Word was made flesh. Thus, we can conclude that Jesus is the Word. Throughout the Word of God, Jesus is lifted up so the Father can be glorified. Jesus is the light of the world. John the Baptist (verse 6) was sent by God to bear witness of that light.

Jesus was born a Jew. In verse 11, it says, "He came unto his own, and his own received him not." His own people rejected Him. Verse 12 tells us, "But as many as received him, to them gave he power to become the sons of God, even to them that believe on his name:" Let's explain how you can become the son of God. In order for you to get to heaven, you must be born again. In John 3:3, Jesus said, "Verily, verily, I say unto thee, Except a man be born again, he cannot see the Kingdom of God." Jesus went on to explain what He meant. All of us are born of a fleshly birth. However, when we trust Jesus as our Lord and Savior, the Spirit of God comes and lives in us. This is the spiritual birth Jesus is talking about.

Now, we must understand what trusting in Jesus as Lord and Savior is all about. Remember this, *you* must do what God says in order to get to heaven. You want to be saved from an eternal Hell. Because of the sin of Adam, we are all born of the flesh—sinners. Jesus paid the price for our sins on the cross of Calvary. Why was Jesus without sin? For His blood was of the Father, who is Holy. The Holy Spirit of God moved upon Mary, and she conceive a child. Therefore, Jesus could not sin, for His blood was of the Father. Remember this, Mary was used by God to carry the Christ-child. Jesus came from heaven, not Mary. Mary was a godly woman God chose to use for His purpose.

Jesus Christ came into this world with a purpose. This purpose was to do the will of His Father. It was the Father's will for Jesus to come and then give His life for all mankind's sins. You may say that you are a pretty good person. You may even say that you do not sin. My friend, God's Word tells us that we are all sinners. Romans 3:23 says, "For all have sinned, and come short of the glory of God." Romans 5:12 says, "Wherefore, as by one man [Adam] sin entered into the world, and death by sin; and so death passed upon all men, for that all have sinned." Now, since we believe the Word of God to be truth, we can plainly see that because of Adam's sin, all are born sinners. Because of Adam's sin, he, Adam and all humanity would die a fleshly death. Therefore, we can conclude that sin brings death. Romans 6:23 says, "For the wages of sin is death; but the gift of God is eternal life through Jesus Christ our Lord."

Because of sin, our body will die. Hebrews 9:27–28 says, "And as it is appointed unto men once to die, but after this the judgment: So Christ was once offered to bear the sins of many; and unto them that look for him shall he appear the second time without sin unto salvation." When Jesus was crucified on the cross, He had all the sins of the world upon Him. Thus, He died for all your past and future sins. Jesus was the supreme sacrifice, for His blood was pure. There is no more need for a sacrifice. Don't let men tell you any different. Before Christ came, sacrifices had to be made according to the way God had told Moses. These sacrifices had to be made each year for the sins of the people.

These sacrifices were made with animals, and their blood was sprinkled upon the mercy seat of God in the tabernacle made for this purpose. The blood of these animals were not pure. That is why the sacrifice had to be done yearly. However, God loved us so much that He sent His only begotten Son to shed His pure and holy blood for our sins. Jesus's blood, as the animals' blood, had to be sprinkled upon the mercy seat of God in the tabernacle in heaven. The tabernacle made on earth was patterned after the tabernacle of heaven. Hebrews 9:23–26 says, "It was therefore necessary that the patterns of things in the heavens should be purified with these; but the heavenly things themselves with better sacrifice than these. For Christ is not entered into the Holy places made with hands, which are the figures of the true; but into heaven itself, now to appear in the presence of God for us: Not yet that he should offer himself often, as the high priest entereth into the holy place every year with blood of others; For them must he often have suffered since the foundation of the world: but now once in the end of the world hath he appeared to put away sin by the sacrifice of himself." The mercy seat of God was located in a place called the holy of holies. There was a vale separating it from the rest of the tabernacle. God used priests, which were from the tribe of Levite. They were the only ones allowed behind this vale to sprinkle the blood of the animals upon the mercy seat of God.

Now, since Jesus made the supreme sacrifice, we have the privilege to accept Him as our Savior. By accepting Him as our Lord and Savior, our spirit is saved from eternal damnation. We will try to explain this to help you to know for sure about you soul. We know, because of the sin of Adam, that our flesh will die and that our spirit is dead already. Our spirit can only be made alive through the Holy Spirit of God. How do we receive the Holy Spirit of God? When you realize that you are a sinner and that you are doomed for hell, then you must repent of your sins with a godly sorrow and ask Jesus to save you—by asking Him into your heart. He, Jesus, can live in you through the Holy Spirit of God. If you ask Jesus to save you and come live in your heart, the Holy Spirit of God will, at that moment, come and abide in you. Remember this, the Father, the Son, and the Holy Ghost are *one*. Therefore, upon salvation, the Holy Spirit comes and abides in you. This makes you a tabernacle of God. Now, you must remember this: God does not fellowship with sin, for *He is holy*. If you want to fellowship with God, you must obey all His Word, for the Word of God says in James 4:17, "Therefore to him that knoweth to do good, and doeth it not, to him it is sin." James 2:10 says, "For whosoever shall keep the whole law, and yet offend in one point, he is guilty of all."

As you can see, you should live the life God wants you to live and not the way you want. By being obedient to God's Word, you will enjoy the blessings of God and the peace that pass all understanding. When you accept Jesus as your Savior, you then are born again spiritually. Then you can call yourself a Christian.

Be sure you have given your all to Jesus if you want to call yourself a Christian. The word *Christian* means to be Christlike. In other words, you are to live as Christ would live today, in this present world, pleasing God in all that you do. Upon the death of Jesus on the cross, the vale was rent from top to bottom by God. God did this so the people would understand that they did not have to go through the priests anymore. People could go to God themselves. They, as we, could go directly to God through our Lord Jesus Christ. For, He is on the right hand of the Father. It is not Mary or Buddha or your mother or dad talking to God for you. It is Jesus, and He alone has that right. For He and He alone died for you on the cross. Jesus is our high priest. After you become a Christian, your Savior, Jesus Christ, pleads for you to the Heavenly Father through His blood when you come to pray to your Heavenly Father. That is why Jesus said we are to ask of the Heavenly Father in Jesus's name. Jesus is our high priest, and we must go to the Father through Jesus. No preacher or priest of today can take the place of Jesus, for Jesus is the only advocate we have to the Heavenly Father.

We hope you are starting to understand what the Word of God is showing you concerning your destination, heaven. In the above paragraphs, you learn that you are born of the flesh, a sinner. Also, you know that you must be born again to enter the kingdom of God. This means, you are to have a spiritual birth. This can only be done when you repent your sins and ask Jesus to come into your heart and save you from eternal hell.

Now, when you repent of your sins, you are telling God that you are sorry for all your sins and that you will not do them anymore. If you have something inside you telling you that you are a sinner and you must get saved or you will go to hell, then you must obey this voice, for this may be your last chance to be saved from going to hell.

As we said before, you must accept the Word of God for what it is: the *truth*. The Bible tells us that you cannot be saved (born again) unless the Father draws you to Himself. This is done by the Holy Spirit of God. John 6:44 says, "No man can come to me except the Father which hath sent me draw him: and I will raise him up at the last day." Jesus said these words. As you see, you must have Jesus for salvation. However, you cannot say you will become a Christian when you decide to. The Holy Spirit of God must draw you to Jesus. You cannot work your way to heaven. Jesus has already paid the price for you and me. He made the supreme sacrifice. There is no more sacrifice for you to make for your sins. With the Holy Spirit of God speaking to your heart about getting saved, you can, by faith, accept Jesus as your Savior. Some may tell you that God has other ways to get to heaven. Do *not* believe this lie. The Word of God is plain. It tells you what you must to do to go to Heaven. There is no other name except Jesus that can save you. Mary cannot save you.

Your preacher cannot save you. Your priest cannot save you. Your mom or dad or sister or brother cannot save you. In Acts 4:12, God says, "Neither is there salvation in any other: for there is none other name under heaven given among men, whereby we must be saved." Jesus said in John 14:6, "I am the way, the truth, and the life, no man cometh unto the father, *but by me.*"

What do we mean by faith? In Hebrews 11, we get the answer to this question. Verse 1 says, "Now faith is the substance of things hoped for, the evidence of things not seen." Faith is taking God at His Word and not doubting Him. Verse 6 says, "But without faith it is impossible to please him: for he that cometh to God must believe that he is, and that he is a rewarder of them that diligently seek him." Ephesians 2:8–9 says, "For by grace are ye saved through faith; and that not of yourselves: it is the gift of God: Not of works, lest any man should boast."

As we said before, you cannot work your way to heaven. Because of the grace of God, we can come to Him through the precious blood of Christ. Grace means unmerited favor. In other words, we do not deserve it, but "for God so loved the world that He gave His only begotten Son, that whosoever believeth in Him should not perish, but have everlasting life" (John 3:16). As you see, God said you cannot be saved by your works. You must have faith in Jesus Christ. You must accept what Jesus did for you 2000 years ago—that He died on the cross, was buried, and after three days, He *rose* from the dead. This is the gospel: the death, the burial, and the resurrection (Corinthians 15:1–4). Romans 10:8–13 says, "The word is nigh thee, even in thy mouth, and in thy heart; that is, the word of faith, which we preach; That if thou shalt confess with thy mouth the Lord Jesus, and shalt believe in thine heart that God hath raised him from the dead, thou shalt be saved. For with the heart man believeth unto righteousness; and with the mouth confession is made unto salvation. For the scripture saith, Whosoever believeth on Him shall not be ashamed. For there is no difference between the Jew and the

Greek: for the same Lord over all is rich unto all that call upon him. For whosoever shall call upon the name of the Lord shall be saved."

Now, you may say that you believe Jesus died, was buried, and rose the third day. Believing that He did this is not enough. Even the devil believes and tremble, but this does not let him go to heaven. James 2:19 says, "Thou believest that there is one God; thou doest well: the devils also believe, and tremble." When a person believes in his heart and repents of his sins and confesses the gospel with his mouth, then he has the right, through the precious blood of Christ, to ask God to save him. Remember this: you cannot be saved in your time. You must hear the Word of God (the Gospel) in order that His Spirit can use the Word to speak to your heart about salvation. Romans 10:17 says, "So then faith cometh by hearing, and hearing by the Word of God." As you read the Gospel, you can hear a voice in your spirit urging you to come to Jesus for salvation.

At this time, you must obey the voice of the Holy Spirit of God if you want to be saved and have everlasting life. Second Corinthians 6:2 says, "Now is the accepted time; behold, now is the day of salvation." The salvation of your soul is very personal. *No one*—I repeat, *no one*—but yourself must answer God at the judgment. Second Corinthians 5:10 says, "For we must all appear before the judgment seat of Christ; that every one may receive the things done in his body, according to that he hath done, whether it be good or bad." Now, upon salvation, you have Christ living in you through His Spirit. So Christ lives in you, and you are to live like Him, pleasing God the Father. Second Corinthians 5:17 says, "Therefore if any man be in Christ, he is a new creature: *old things are passed away; behold, all things are become new.*"

As you see, after you accept Jesus as your Savior and ask him into your heart, then you are to be a different person. If you truly repented your sins, then you were telling God that you would not go back to those sins anymore.

You can see that if the Holy Spirit of God, which does not fellowship with sin, abides in you, then you are to strive not to let sin come into your life. A word of caution: you cannot overcome sin on your own. You and I must always depend on God for the strength to fight the darts of Satan. In order for you to know how to overcome Satan, you must study the Word of God faithfully. Second Timothy 2:15 says, "Study to show thyself approved unto God, a workman that needeth to be ashamed, rightly divided the Word of Truth."

As we said before, your works will not get you to heaven. However, after you are born again into the family of God, then you are to do good works for His glory. Ephesians 2:10 says, "For we are his workmanship, created in Christ Jesus unto good works, which God hath before ordained that we should walk in them." First Corinthians 10:31 says, "Whether therefore ye eat, or drink, or whatsoever ye do, do all the glory of God." When Jesus was on this earth, He did all to the glory of the Father. Since Jesus lives in us, we are to try to live like Him and do all that we do for the Glory of God.

Satan leads many people to believe his lies. In Satan's sly ways, he can make lies so close to the truth that many will follow his directions. It is my prayer that you will seek the real truth, Jesus, through His Word. Doesn't it make sense to follow the way of Jesus since He will be the One to judge you? You cannot know the way unless you know Jesus personally, for He is the way, the truth, and the life. Do you not realize that without Jesus, you are dead spiritually?

Let us look at what Apostle Paul wrote to the Christians at the church of Ephesus. Ephesians 2:1–7 says, "And you hath he quickened, who were dead in trespasses and sins; wherein in time past ye walked according to the course of this world, according to the prince of the power of the air, the spirit that now worketh in the children of disobedience: Among whom also we all had our conversation in times past in the lusts of our flesh, fulfilling the desires of the flesh and of the mind; and were by nature the children of wrath, even as others. But God, who is rich in mercy, for his great love wherewith he loved us, Even when we were dead in sins hath quickened us together with Christ (*by grace ye are saved*) And hath raised us up together, and made us sit together in heavenly places in Christ Jesus: That in the ages to come he might show the exceeding riches of his grace in his kindness towards us through Christ Jesus."

Paul is reminding the Christians what they were before they were saved, and where they are now. You must know where you came from and where you are going. In verse 1, we see that God quickened us. In other words, we are made alive upon salvation. Why should we be made alive? We should be made alive because we were spiritually dead in our sins.

Remember, because of Adam, we are all born sinners, and our soul is doomed for hell without trusting in Jesus. Therefore, as we looked at the Word of God, we found that there is no other way to get to heaven but by Jesus. For we know that the Word of God tells us that Jesus is the way, the truth, and the life; and no man comes to the Father but by Him.

My friend, we want you to understand that religion, churches, priests, preachers, teachers, family, friends, or any other person cannot answer to God for you. Even the many great men and women of the Bible cannot help you. This includes Mary, Apostle Paul, Peter, James, John, Moses, and anyone else that you may want to name. These individuals have to answer to God for themselves, just as you and me. *You* and *you* alone must make the decision, which is the most important one of your life. This decision is either to accept Jesus Christ as your Lord and Savior or deny Him and suffer eternal judgment. In order for you to have the peace that pass all understanding, you must put God *first* in your life, others *second*, and yourself third.

Jesus was asked what was the greatest commandment. His reply was "Thou shalt love the Lord thy God with all thy heart, and with all thy soul, and with all thy mind. This is the first and great commandment. And the second is like unto it; Thou shalt love thy neighbor as thyself. On these two commandments hang all the law and the prophets" (Matthew 22:37–40). Is this the goal of your life? Or do you not take God seriously? You better. You may not even fear God. You better. In Matthew 10:26–33, the Word of God says,

> Fear them not therefore: for there is nothing covered, that shall not be revealed; and hid, that shall not be known. What I tell you in darkness, that speak ye in light: and what ye hear in the ear, that preach ye upon the house tops. And fear not them which kill the body, but are not able to kill the

> soul: but rather fear him which is able to destroy both soul and body in hell. Are not two sparrows sold for a farthing? and one of them shall not fall on the ground without your Father. But the very hairs of your head are all numbered. Fear ye not therefore, ye are more value than many sparrows. Whosoever therefore shall confess me before men, him will I confess also before my Father which is in heaven. But whosoever shall deny me before men, him will I also deny before my Father which is in heaven.

Jesus was telling His disciples some very important things in these above verses. If we are to be one of His disciples, we must heed to His words.

You can go through this life with peace in your heart if you put God first. You will have many setbacks, but God's grace is sufficient for you and me. We will have much tribulation in this world. However, Jesus said in John 16:33, "These things I have spoken unto you, that in me ye might have peace. In the world ye shall have tribulation: but be of good cheer; I have overcome the world."

It is my prayer that you will humble your heart before God and become an obedient child of His so you can know where you came from and you may know where you are going. First John 5:13 says, "These things have I written unto you that believe on the name of the Son of God; that ye may know that ye have eternal life."

You want to go to heaven. Are you willing to follow God's road map to heaven? Do you want God to lead you all the way? Do you want to give yourself to Him? God loves you and wants to show you the way to heaven. God will not force Himself on you. Jesus stands at your heart's door and knocks. He will not force the door open. You must open your heart's door from the inside of your heart.

Time is short on this earth. What we do in our lives depend on ourselves. If we follow Jesus, we will overcome any obstacle that befall us. This walk with Jesus must be done on a moment-by-moment basis. He never leaves us. Sometimes, as we travel in this life, we may stray off His directions and suffer more. But Jesus loves us so much that He is just to forgive us our sins if we repent and confess them to Him. If we love Jesus, we will not continue in sin. If we truly love God, we will strive to please our Heavenly Father in all things.

Remember this: Whether we eat or drink or do whatsoever, we should do them for the glory of God. Why? For our life is short. James 4:14–17 says, "Whereas ye know not what shall be on the morrow. For what is your life? It is even a vapor, that appeareth for a little time, and then vanisheth away. For that ye ought to say, If the Lord will, we shall live, and do this, or that. But now ye rejoice in your boastings: all such rejoicing is evil. Therefore to him that knoweth to do good and doeth it not, to him it is sin."

May God use you all the days of your life for His Glory.

Bro. Roger D. Cole

PEACE WITH GOD

Introduction

My friend, before studying this lesson, please read this: "He that refuseth instruction despiseth his own soul: but he that heareth reproof getteth understanding. The fear of the Lord is the instruction of wisdom; and before honor is humility" (Proverbs 15:32–33). Please read the verses two more times.

Whether you are a Christian (born again) or not, you will pay the cost for not obeying the leadership of the Holy Spirit to come to God for salvation. Stop reading and fall on your knees, repent your sins, and accept Jesus as your Lord and Savior. Christian friend, if the Holy Spirit moves upon you about unconfessed sins in your heart, I urge you to grieve not the Holy Spirit and repent your sins so you may get back into fellowship with God. Remember this: God does not fellowship with sin.

We must worship God in spirit and truth, for He is truth. As you study this lesson, you will notice that we have many scripture references for you to get a deeper look at what we are trying to relate to you. Scripture is to be interpreted with scripture. Therefore, do not take for granted that everything one says is the truth. Search the scriptures that you may be able to try the spirits, whether they be of God or not (1 John 4:1–6). Sometimes it is necessary to study a complete chapter or even more to get the full meaning of what God is telling us. Remember, the Word of God does not contradict itself. God doesn't lie, for He is truth. God is not that author of confusion

(1 Corinthians 14:33). We caution you to not take scripture out of text to suit your own will.

We should always strive moment by moment to obey the will of God in our lives. My friend, you cannot please God by living for Him at your convenience. To walk with Jesus is most rewarding. This walk must be a daily walk if we are going to have peace of God that passes all understanding (Philippians 4:7).

In order to have this peace of God, we must make peace with God. We must depend on Jesus's strength to help us surrender our all to God. We can do all things through Christ (Philippians 4:13). Please understand that you cannot have true peace with God if there is any sin in your heart. All that we do should be to the glory of God. First Corinthians 10:31 say, "Whether therefore ye eat, or drink, or whatsoever ye do, do all to the glory of God."

Remember this: do not try to measure your sin. God already has. If you have broken one commandment, you are guilty of all (James 2:10–13).

Are you willing to do what God wants you to do to come to the place where you have real peace with God? When you do come to have this peace, you will be a different person. You will let the Holy Spirit of God lead you in all things with joy and peace in your heart.

You may say, "I am good enough already to please God." My prayer is you are walking close to Jesus every day. My friend, God's word says, "There is none righteous, no not one" (Romans 3:10). In Romans 3:23 we see, "For all have sinned, and come short of the glory of God." Do not ever think that you cannot sin. As long as you have this fleshly body, when you are not in the spirit, you can yield to temptation. Hebrews 11:6 says, "But without faith it is impossible to please him: for he that cometh to God must believe that he is, and that he is a rewarder of them that diligently seek him."

Dearly beloved, for you to enjoy walking with Jesus, you must learn not walk by sight but by faith. Read Romans 1:16–19. Be not ashamed of the gospel of Christ, for you hold the truth in unrighteousness that God, through the Holy Spirit, has showed you. Therefore, as a Christian, we should live by faith.

Throughout the world, we hear the talk of world peace. Beware, our redemption draws nigh. Read these scriptures: 1 Thessalonians 4:1–18, 1 Thessalonians 5:13, and Matthew 21:28. This world knows not the Prince of Peace, our Lord and Savior, Jesus Christ. This world is striving to have a one-world government. This will come to pass to fulfill the Word of God. These nations may use God or Christian ethics as the reason to have world peace. In order to control world peace, there must be a one-world government, such as the United Nations. *Beware* my friend when you hear that we have a new world order. When this government is in full control over all world matters, then it will be too late for people to overthrow it. The stage is being set for what all the Antichrist spoke of in the Word of God. The world will not have true peace until the Prince of Peace reigns here in person.

Dearly beloved, time as we know it is very short. If we are to do anything for God, we must get busy *now*. Do you want your friends, relatives, and all the people you know go to hell? Of course, you don't. You can make the difference in many lives if you begin to show the love you have for God in your life. Who careth for my soul? Lovest thou me? Do you really love *Jesus* (John 21:15–17)?

Remember, the peace of this world being talked about is a false peace. Christian friend, you live in this world, but your citizenship is in heaven (Ephesians 2:6, Philippians 3:20). You are not of this world; therefore, you can truly have the peace of God that passes all understanding (Philippians 4:7).

There has been much prayer and study in preparing this lesson for you. May Jesus be lifted up that you may be drawn nearer to Him as you study His Word.

In today's world, we see people rushing to and fro. It seems as if one might meet themselves coming and going. Man has advanced so much in technology that he is caught up right in the middle of things. It seems that one is pressured to go with the flow of things. It need not be so. People of today's generation are spoiled with the conveniences of life. We, especially Americans, have learned to live by sight to survive or get ahead in today's world. We, as Christians, have missed so much of God's blessings by not learning to live by

His faith. Thank God for the many conveniences we have. However, it seems that people are never satisfied. The more we have, the more we want. It seems that most of us allow ourselves to get in a financial bind and blame God for letting this happen. Whenever you take your eyes off Jesus, you will suffer with the problems you create. Times are hard today. Things will get worse as the return of our Lord comes near. However, we can endure to the end if we depend on Him for our needs. He will always provide if we do our part as a Christian. Henceforth, we can still have joy during these times as we look for His coming appearance.

My friend, God wants His children (born-again believers) to be drawn closer and closer to Him. Never forget, God is in control of all situations. As you grow spiritually and love God with all your heart, you will understand the meaning of Romans 8:28. He allows many things to happen in our lives so that we may learn and grow spiritually and that we may be able to help others.

As Christians, we must put God first, others second, and ourselves last. With an obedient, humble heart meeting this in order, we are on our way to a victorious, abundant Christian life.

You may say your family comes first. You may say your church comes first. Nothing should come before God. The Lord was asked, "What was the greatest commandment?" Matthew 22:37–40 says, "Jesus said unto him, Thou shalt love the Lord thy God with all thy heart, and with all thy soul, and with all mind. And the second is like unto it, Thou shalt love thy neighbor as thyself. On these two commandments hang all the law and the prophets."

You must not forget that you would have nothing in this world if God would not allow you to have it. He wants to bless you. He wants you to glorify Him with what He has given you. Whether it be talents or material blessings. Do you give Him the glory in all that you have? He loves you. He proved it on the cross, having His only begotten Son die the sin death for you. Throughout the Word of God, you can see where men were blessed, not only spiritually, but also physically with families and wealth when they served God faithfully. When we say faithfully, we mean by God's standard, not man's. God's standard is plain and simple if you study His Word daily and allow the Holy Spirit of God to lead you in all things. As a Christian, we are to be sure that God will supply all our needs if we love Him (Philippians 4:19). If we love Him, we will strive to do His will for our lives as the Spirit leads. Therewith, we can be as the apostle Paul, content (Philippians 4:1–13).

My friend, if you know not Jesus as your Lord and Savior, you must know this: you *cannot* pick the time for you to be saved (born again). God's Word is explained. John 6:44 says, "No man can come to me, except the Father hath sent me draw him." Romans 10:17 says, "Faith cometh by hearing and hearing by the Word of God." By hearing or reading the Word of God, the Holy Spirit will or already has moved upon your heart to accept Jesus as Lord and Savior. Whenever the Holy Spirit moves upon you to do so, you should do so immediately, for this may be your last chance. *You* must realize that salvation is free, for Jesus paid it all for you and me. Only by the grace of God can we be saved through faith in Jesus Christ, who shed His sinless blood for you and me. Ephesians 2:8–9 says, "For by grace are ye saved, through faith; and that not of yourselves: it is the gift of God: Not of works, lest any man should boast."

Peace with God

Checkup Time

Are you a member of a church? Do you go faithfully to this church? Is Jesus being lifted up in the services at this church? Are you the kind of person that feels like you have done your duty by going to church on Sunday? Maybe you belong to a church that has two services on Sunday and one on Wednesday, and you attend all three. Do you go to church because you love Jesus and want to please Him? Are you really pleased with yourself in your service to God? Do you think you are doing enough for Jesus? What are your priorities in life? Does your job or your girlfriend or boyfriend come first? Does your wife or family come first? Do you have joy and peace in your heart about your relationship to God?

In order for you or me to know where we are going with Jesus, we must analyze where we are now. Only you can answer the questions for yourself. When was the last time you told some dear soul about the saving power of Jesus's precious blood that was shed for you and me? Do you dress like a Christian or dress like the world wants you to? Do you talk like a Christian should or talk like the people of the world? Do you influence people in the godly way, or does their influence controls you? Have you been faithful in the studying of God's Word? Have you been faithful in your prayer life? Have you been faithful in your tithes and offerings to God? What kind of church would your church be if all the members were like you?

On your everyday job, you surely must try to do your best, hoping that you will get a good report from your superiors to enhance the chances for a raise or advancement. As a Christian, we must try to do our best with all the talents the Lord has given us to serve Him. We should desire to have a good report as He looks upon our lives. Too many Christians want to reap the rewards from God without the work for God. Are you struggling through life not knowing if you will ever make it financially or ever be happy spiritually? If your answer is yes to this question, then, my friend, it is *checkup time.*

It is our prayer that we can help you know where you are with God and where you are going with God. Please remember that no one but yourself is responsible to listen to God as He speaks to you through His Word and to respond as the Holy Spirit moves in your heart. You must act immediately in a positive way if you want to have the joy and peace you desire for your life.

Notice that we refer to you many times to Romans 14:11–12. We see that everyone must give an account to God of what they do on earth, whether good or bad. God created us with a free will. This means, you can either serve God and reap the rewards or not serve Him and reap the wrath of God. The choice is yours. Remember what Ephesians 2:10 says: "For we are his workmanship, created in Christ Jesus unto good works, which God hath before ordained that we should walk in them."

You cannot play both sides of the fence. It will catch up with you, and you will suffer much pain. Matthew 6:24 says, "No man can serve two masters: for either he will hate the one, and love the other; or else he will hold to the one, and despise the other. Ye cannot serve God and mammon." My beloved, read the rest of Matthew chapter 6. You will notice that Jesus is telling us to put our priorities in the right place. We should not be worrying about tomorrow, what we shall eat, or what we shall drink. We must learn to live by faith. If we seek the things of God *first* in our lives and seek His righteousness, then all these other things will be added unto us.

Peace with God

Christian or What?

Many people in this world have a misconception of what a Christian is. Some say they were born a Christian. Others may say, "I belong to this church or that church, therefore I am a Christian." Yet others say, "I had an unusual experience in my life, such as a close encounter with death. Consequently, I am a Christian." Then some say, "I am a good person, therefore I feel like I will go to heaven. So I guess I am a Christian."

We could give many examples. However, we want to get to the truth of this subject.

There is only one way to understand the truth. This is through the Holy Scriptures, given *for* man *by* GOD *through* men, as the Holy Spirit told them to write. Read 2 Peter 1:21. These scriptures are the Living Word of God. In Revelation 22:18–19, we are told not add to the Holy Scriptures or take away from the Holy Scriptures. Therefore, we are to accept God's Word as it is.

Where did the word *Christian* come from? In the book of Isaiah 62:2, we see that God prophesies approximately seven hundred years before the birth of Christ that His people shall be called by a new name. In chapter 65:15, God tells us that He will call His servants by another name. The Jews were God's chosen people. All other people were called Gentiles. Hence, whether one is a Jew or a Gentile, he is called a Christian if he is a born-again believer. A born-again believer is a follower of Christ. Therefore, we are His disciples. Consequently, we are to be called Christians. Looking in the book of Acts, we see in verse 26 of chapter 11 that "the disciples were called Christians first in Antioch."

Who were the disciples? They were men that Jesus personally called out publicly to follow Him. These twelve men walked with Jesus approximately three years. One of these twelve betrayed Him with a kiss (Matthew 26:46–49). After Jesus's resurrection, He met with His disciples and gave them a command. This command is meant for all His followers (disciples) throughout the ages. We read in Matthew 28:18–20, "And Jesus came and spake unto them, saying, All power is given unto me in heaven and in earth. Go ye therefore, and teach all nations, baptizing them in the name of the Father, and of the Son, and of the Holy Ghost; Teaching them to observe all things whatsoever I have commanded you; and, lo I am with you always, even unto the end of the world."

Upon Jesus's ascension, the disciples had Him no more in body. But Jesus told them that He would send them a comforter, the Holy Spirit of God, to live in them forever (John 14:15–17).

We, as Christians, must realize what we are supposed to be. The word *Christian* is simple. It means to be like Christ. In other words, we are to live our lives as Christ Himself would live in the world today, pleasing His Father in all things.

Read Romans 5:6–11. We see that Christ died for the ungodly. This includes you and me. "God commendeth his love towards us, in that, while we were yet sinners, Christ died for us." We are justified by His blood. The atonement was made for us through our Lord and Savior Jesus Christ. Therefore, you were bought with a price, the precious blood of Jesus. We belong to Him. This means that Jesus should not only be our Savior but also our Lord and Master.

As Savior, Jesus has paid the sin death for you and me and has saved us from eternal hell.

As Lord of our lives, we understand that our whole being, body, soul, and mind belongs to Him. Therefore, we should desire to learn all about Him so we may be able to worship and praise Him daily.

As our Master, we will obey each and every command to the fullness. This includes not only what His Word says to do and what not to do, but also obeying God as His Spirit leads us in our lives daily. Even though we may not understand at first, if we obey His will by faith, then we will be blessed. This will allow us to become stronger and stronger in the Lord. Henceforth, we will have a closer walk with Him. We will have that peace that passes all understanding. Are you seeking this peace in your life?

If we truly repented our sins and accepted Jesus Christ as our Lord and Savior, then we are new creatures in Christ Jesus (Romans 10:9–13 and 2 Corinthians 5:17). Do we understand what repentance means? To repent one's sins, we must first realize that we have sinned against God. Then we must come to God with a humble, contrite heart seeking His mercy and forgiveness. If we don't have a godly sorrow for our sins, then we are just playing games, and we are not serious with God. Romans 3:23 says, "For all have sinned, and come short of the glory of God." If we come to God in the spirit of humility, we are saying that we are willing to do what He wants us to do so that we may have peace with Him.

My Christian friend, upon salvation, we have the Holy Spirit of God come and abide in us. Therefore, we have Jesus living in us through the Holy Spirit of God. Since God lives in us, we are the tabernacle of God. Let us look at Ephesians 2:1–7:

> And you hath he quickened, who were dead in trespasses and sins; Wherein in time past ye walked according to the course of this world., according to the prince of the air, the spirit that now worketh in the children of disobedience: Among whom also we all had our conversation in times past in the lusts of our flesh, fulfilling the desires of the flesh and of the mind; and were by nature the children of wrath, even as others. But God, who is rich in mercy, for His great love herewith he loved us, Even when we were dead in sins hath quickened us together with Christ, (by grace ye are saved;) And hath raised us up together, and made us sit together in heavenly places in Christ Jesus: That in the ages to come

> He might show the exceeding riches of his grace
> in his kindness toward us through Christ Jesus.

My dearly beloved, as a Christian, you surely realize what you were, walking to the course of this world, fulfilling the desires of the flesh and of the mind. As a Christian, you know that you have a new nature, and your desires are changed to do godly things instead of worldly things. Remember this: you live in this world, but you are not of this world. Don't let worldly pressures cause you to take your eyes off Jesus. If you take your eyes off Jesus, then you will suffer more. Remember, Peter asked our Lord to let him come and meet Jesus on the water. Jesus allowed Peter to do so. As Peter was walking on the water, he took his eyes off Jesus and noticed the strong winds and was afraid and began to sink. Then Peter did as all of us do when we get ourselves in a mess: he cried, "Lord, save me!" (Matthew 14:29–3). We hope and pray that God can look at your life and say, "My child of faith."

You understand that upon salvation, the Holy Spirit of God comes and abides in you. Consequently, since God lives in us through His Spirit, then we are the tabernacle of God. What great joy and responsibility this bestows upon us. Do you understand that God goes with us everywhere we go? Do you think God is pleased with places you take Him? Is everything you say or think pleasing to God? Have you been feeding your mind with the things of this world, or have you been feasting upon the Word of God? Ask yourself, "Would Jesus go to the places I go? Would Jesus do the things I do? Would Jesus say and think the things I say and think?" Remember this: if there is any doubt whether Jesus would go, do, say, or think the things you do, then you should repent and ask God to forgive you and to help you overcome these problems through His Word. Remember, my friend, Jesus gave glory to the Father in all things. This is to be our goal as a Christian. For a Christian is to be Christlike.

My beloved, we cannot achieve this goal until we discipline ourselves to lay aside the things of this world and begin a faithful, daily study of the Word of God. We must feed the spiritual part of our being with spiritual food, which is the Word of God. You can go to all the revival meetings you want to. You may attend many seminars and listen to great men of God. But no one can teach you better than the Holy Spirit of God, for He is to teach us all things of Christ through His Word. You may have a college degree of some sort. But you cannot always depend on your teachers, pastors, or friends to give the truth of things pertaining to the Word of God. We must study to show ourselves approved unto God, a workman that need not to be ashamed, rightly dividing the word of truth (2 Timothy 2:15). Let's let the Holy Spirit of God do the work He was sent to do. Let's not grieve the Holy Spirit of God that we may enjoy the fullness of our salvation. Ephesians 4:29–30 says, "Let no corrupt communication proceed out of your mouth, but that which is good to the use of edifying, that it may minister grace unto the hearers. And grieve not the Holy Spirit of God, whereby ye are sealed unto the day of redemption."

Christian friend, do you want to face the truth or not? Will you do what is necessary to improve your relationship with our Heavenly Father? Do you want the full salvation? Remember this: God does not fellowship with sin (1 John 1:1–9). We see that God does forgive a true repented heart of sin. In Proverbs 28:6–14, we see in verse 6, "Better is the poor that walketh in his righteousness, than he that is perverse in his ways, though he be rich." Verse 7 says, "Whoso keepeth the law is a wise son: but he that is companion of riotous men shameth his father." My friend, be very careful with your soul. Listen to the Word of God. Verse 9 of chapter 28 says, "He that turneth away his ear from hearing the law [in other words, the Word of God] even his prayer shall be abomination." Let us look at verses 13 and 14 of Proverbs 28:

> He that covereth his sins shall not prosper; but whoso confesseth and forsaketh them shall have mercy. Happy is the man that feareth always; but he that hardeneth his heart shall fall into mischief.

In John 14:6, Jesus said, "I am the way, the truth, and the life; no man cometh to the Father but by me." John 1:1 says, "In the beginning was the *Word*, and the *Word* was with God, and the *Word* was God." John 1:14 says, "And the *Word* was made flesh, and dwelt among us (and we beheld His glory, and the glory as of the only begotten of the Father), full of grace and *truth*."

As we can see, Jesus *is* the Word; Jesus is truth; and Jesus is the only begotten Son of God. "For God so loved the world, that he gave his only begotten Son, that whosoever believeth in him should not perish, but have everlasting life" (John 3:16).

Before Jesus came to earth in the form of man, born of a virgin, whose seed was implanted in Mary by the Holy Spirit of God, God had given Moses the order in which the people of God were to bring sacrifices for the covering of their sins. Sacrifices were made by the high priests. The blood from these sacrificed animals was sprinkled upon the mercy seat of God, which was located behind the curtain of the holy of holies. When the supreme sacrifice was made on Mount Calvary for the sins of the whole world, the curtain to the holy of holies was rent from the top to the bottom. This is one of God's way of telling us that man did not have to make any more sacrifices—as before with the high priest going into the holy of holies to sprinkle blood upon the mercy seat of God—for we have a new high priest: Jesus Christ, who took His blood into heaven and sprinkled His blood upon the mercy seat of God. You and I can go directly to our Heavenly Father through our High Priest, Jesus Christ, who is sitting on the right hand of the Father. Read Hebrews 8:1 and Romans 8:34. We know that Jesus is at the right hand of the Father, making intercession for you and me. It is not Mary or Abraham or Buddha or the pope. Jesus lives in us through the Holy Spirit of God; for the Father, the Son, and the Holy Spirit are one Godhead. Read Acts 17:29, Romans 1:20, Colossians 2:6–10, and 1 John 5:1–9.

God took the fleshly Word into heaven but left us the written Living Word. Gods uses His Word to speak to us through the workings of the Holy Spirit. If we realize that we have all the resources available to us to live a victorious Christian life, we can do great things for God. Christian friend, do you want to know the will of God for your life? Of course you do. Is your heart right with God at this very moment? If not, heed to His Spirit *now*.

Peace with God

Salvation

I

Upon salvation, there are certain things that are expected of you. You should first follow the Lord in baptism. Acts 2:41 says, "Then they that gladly receive his words were baptized." Baptism by immersion pictures our position with Christ in His death, burial, and resurrection.

Next, you are to find a Bible-believing, Bible-teaching New Testament church. A church that uses the King James Version, which has stood the test of time throughout the ages.

Upon salvation, you are to be a witness for Christ. You should not be ashamed of your Savior. Mark 8:34–38 says, "And when he had called the people unto him with his disciples also, he said unto them, Whosoever will come after me, let him deny himself, and take up his cross, and follow me. For whosoever shall lose his life for my sake and the gospel's, the same shall save it. For what shall it profit a man, if he shall gain the whole world, and lose his own soul? Or what shall a man give in exchange for his soul? Whosoever therefore shall be ashamed of me and of my words in this adulterous and sinful generation; of him also shall the Son of man be ashamed, when he cometh in the glory of his Father with the holy angels."

Upon salvation, you should serve sin no more. Read Romans 6:1–9. This is a major part of your witness. Second Corinthians 5:17

says, "Therefore, if any man be in Christ, he has a new creature: old things are passed away; behold, all things are become new." Your wants and desires should be different. You should want to do good and have good thoughts, not bad. Remember this: Jesus Christ loved you so much that He died on the cross of Calvary for your sins. The least you can do for Him is to love Him enough to live for Him. You can only achieve this by the leadership of the Holy Spirit of God, who comes and abides in you when you ask Jesus to come into your heart and save your soul from an eternal hell.

II

You must study the Word of God faithfully. Second Timothy 2:15 says, "Study to show thyself approved unto God, a workman that needeth not to be ashamed, rightly dividing the word of truth." Don't be afraid that you will not understand the Word of God. If you do your part to study the Word of God, He, through the Holy Spirit, will show you what you need to know from day to day.

Now since the Holy Spirit lives in you, you must realize that God does not fellowship with sin. Make sure you heart is right with God before you begin to study the Word of God. This will enable you to fellowship with Him as you read His Word. This will enable you to be receptive to the Holy Spirit speaking to you through the Word of God.

This should be your desire. First Peter 2:2 says, "As newborn babes, desire the sincere milk of the word, that ye may grow thereby." As you grow in the Lord, you will get stronger in Him. Caution: do not try to eat the steak of the Word when you cannot yet digest the milk of the Word. Live the Word as revealed to you. God will always show you what you need day by day. Proverbs 27:1 says, "Boast not thyself of tomorrow; for thou knowest not what a day may bring forth." God knows what will be tomorrow. Therefore, He knows what you need better than you do yourself. God has chosen you to be a soldier in His army. Second Timothy 2:1–4 says, "Thou therefore, my son, be strong in the grace that is in Christ Jesus. And the things that thou hast heard of me among many witnesses, the same commit thou to faithful men, who shall be able to teach others also. Thou therefore endure hardness, as a good soldier of Jesus Christ. No man that warreth entangleth himself with the affairs of this life; that he may please him who hath chosen him to be a soldier."

Take time out of busy life to let your Heavenly Father speak to you. If you want the peace of God that passes all understanding, you must discipline yourself to study the Word of God on a daily basis. Be patient; don't rush God. You will grow according to your eating of the Word and living of what you eat. In other words, you must digest what the Holy Spirit has showed you before He will feed you more spiritual food.

When studying the Word of God, you must study in a systematic and orderly manner. Only then will you get the most out of your studying. First Corinthians 14:40 says, "Let all things be done decently and in order." We would like to suggest that you read one chapter of the book of Proverbs each morning before beginning your day. The first chapter to be read on the first day of the month, and the second chapter on the second day of the month, and so on. You will gain much wisdom and common sense from this book.

Pray faithfully. God has talked to you from His Word through the Holy Spirit. Now since you are one of His sons, you can come to the throne of grace and speak to your Heavenly Father. Before you do so, you must be sure your heart is completely honest before God. Hebrews 4:13–16 says, "Neither is there any creature that is not manifest in his sight; but all things are *naked* and *opened* unto the eyes of him with whom we have to do. Seeing then that we have a great priest, that is passed into the heavens, Jesus the Son of God, let us hold fast our profession. For we have not a high priest which cannot be touched with the feeling of our infirmities; but was in all points tempted like as we are, yet without sin. Let us therefore come boldly unto the throne of grace, that we may obtain mercy, and find grace to help in time of need."

God desires you and me to bring our petitions before Him in prayer, even though He already knows our needs and our desires. This is part of His perfect plans for His children: to let our petition be brought to Him ourselves. How often do you talk to Him? Do you pray only when in need? Or do you visit with Him in prayer to praise and thank Him for what He has done and is doing in your life?

Remember, if sin is in your life, repent and be right with God before you bring your petitions to Him. Sometimes, you may not know how to pray. Have no fear. The Holy Spirit of God will help you if you seek His help. Romans 8:26–27 says, "Likewise the Spirit also helpeth our infirmities: for we know not what we should pray for as we ought: but the Spirit itself maketh intercession for us with groanings which cannot be uttered. And he that searcheth the hearts knoweth what is the mind of the Spirit, because he maketh intercession for the saints according to The will of God."

III

Serve Jesus. As you grow in the Lord, you will have opportunities to serve Him more. As a newborn Christian, you are to be faithful to the house of God. You are to join a church that the Holy Spirit of God will lead you to. This church should preach and teach the Word of God as it is, not wavering from the truth as many do. Second Timothy 3:1–7 says, "This know also, that in the last days perilous times shall come. For men shall be lovers of their own selves, covetous, boasters, proud, blasphemers, disobedient to parents, unthankful, unholy, Without natural affection, trucebreakers false accusers, incontinent, fierce, despisers of those that are good, Traitors, heady, high-minded, lovers of pleasures more than lovers of God; Having a form of godliness, but denying the power thereof: *from such turn away*. For of this sort are they which creep in houses, and lead captive silly women laden with sins, led away with divers lusts, Ever learning, and never able to come to the knowledge of the truth." This church must teach the gospel, which is the *death*, *burial*, and *resurrection* of our Lord and Savior, Jesus Christ (1 Corinthians 15:1–4). This church must also teach the *virgin birth* of Christ Jesus. Read Isaiah 7:14 and Matthew 1:23 and Luke 1:27. This church must teach the *new birth* in Christ Jesus, which is a spiritual birth (John 3:3).

Upon accepting Jesus Christ as your Lord and Savior, the Holy Spirit of God comes and abides in you. If any church you belong to

FEASTING ON THE LIVING WORD OF GOD

does not teach the above, then you should pray for God's guidance as to where He would have you move your membership.

Please continue reading. This will help you to know more about God's will for your life.

Peace with God

The apostle Paul wrote two letters to the church of Corinth. Remember, a local New Testament church consists of a group of baptized believers. Consequently, we see that Paul is writing to Christians. Some of these Christians have allowed sin to creep into their lives. Paul is very straight to the point in letting the church know their responsibilities about the situation. Christian friend, please remember that, as a member of your church, you are a part of the body. Therefore, what you do as a Christian, affects the whole church in a positive or negative way. Please realize how important you are to the church body. Christians today have a tendency to live the life they want with no serious thought of the rest of the church body. Be honest with yourself. You would not take a hammer and hit your little finger on purpose, would you? Would this glorify Christ? Now when you do something in your life that would cause hurt to another church member, you would be doing harm to yourself as well, for you all are part of the same body.

One of the greatest weapons Satan uses in the church is your tongue. If Satan can get your mind on someone else, then you can be his pawn to move about as he wishes to accomplish what he wants you to do. As a Christian, we must keep our minds on Jesus and the things of God if we are to live a life pleasing to God. Be aware that Satan wants you to compare your Christian life to someone else's instead of comparing your life to Jesus's.

Remember this: God's Word never changes. Just because modern churches do as pleasing to man, this does not make it right with God. So many preachers and teachers today are self-called and not God-called. They have their reward of being seen by men. Yet many are God-called and have left their first love, Jesus. They let influencing people control their service to God. Therefore, they have to suffer the consequences.

My beloved, be sure that the man you follow is following Jesus. Does he love as Jesus does with no respect of persons? Does he study the Word of God faithfully? Does he live what he preaches? Is God first in his life? Does he believe that the Word of God (King James Version) is without error? In all these, the greatest is love. Yet we must understand that man of God is still human. But if we work together in love, we can overcome all obstacles that Satan may put before us, and Jesus will be lifted up. If we are to be the church we are supposed to be, then we must seek to do all things God's way.

Let us look at 1 Corinthians 6:9–20:

> Know ye not that the unrighteous shall not inherit the Kingdom of God? Be not deceived: neither fornicators, nor idolaters, nor adulterers, nor effeminate, nor abusers of themselves with mankind, Nor thieves, nor covetous, nor drunkards, nor revilers, nor extortioners, shall inherit the Kingdom of God. And such were some of you: but ye are washed, but ye are sanctified, but ye are justified in the name of the Lord Jesus, and by the Spirit of our God. All things are lawful unto me, but all things are not expedient: all things are lawful for me, but I will not be brought under the power of any. Meats for the belly, and belly for meats: but God shall destroy both it and them. Now, the body is not for fornication, but for the Lord; and the Lord for the body. And God hath both raised up the Lord, and will also raise up us by his own power. Know ye not that your bodies are the members of Christ? Shall I then take the members of Christ, and make them the members of a harlot? God forbid. What? Know ye not that he which is joined to a harlot is one body? For two, saith he, shall be one flesh. But

> he that is joined unto the Lord is one spirit. Flee fornication. Every sin that a man doeth is without the body; but he that committeth fornication sinneth against his own body. What? Know ye not that your body is the temple of the holy Ghost which is in you, which ye have of God, and ye are not your own? For ye are brought with a price: therefore glorify God in your body, and your spirit, which are God's.

For you may say that you can control sin in your life. You are wrong. Proverbs 6:27 says, "Can a man take fire in his bosom, and his clothes not be burned?" Sin is like a cancer, if it is not removed completely, it will spread. If allowed to go unchecked, then at some time, it will consume you, and the end is death. Whatever sin you may have in your life, whether large or small in your eyes, must be confessed to God with a repentant heart. This will allow you to fellowship with your Heavenly Father. However, if you are one that continues to grieve the Holy Spirit, you will never have the peace with God that passes all understanding. Numbers 32:23 says, "But if ye will not do so, behold, ye have sinned against the Lord: and be sure your sin will find you out." Galatians 6:7 says, "Be not deceived; God is not mocked: for whatsoever a man soweth, that shall he also reap."

My beloved, don't be deceived by Satan's vises. You will never have the full joy of your salvation if you continue playing with sin. Read Psalm 51. You can see what David did. He realized he sinned against God (verses 1–5).

David saw that God desired truth in the inward parts of man. David knew that only God could forgive him of his sins and make his heart clean (verses 6–10) David wanted the joy of his salvation restored unto him (verse 12). We must remember that our salvation is the Lord's, for He died for us. After David was restored his joy, he was able to teach transgressors God's ways, and sinners could be converted unto God (verse 13).

My prayer is that you want this for your life. If you do so, then you can become wise. Proverbs 11:30 says, "The fruit of the righteous is a tree of life; and he that winneth souls is wise." Are you bearing fruit? Do you want to become wiser in the Lord? You can if you put God first in your life.

Ephesians 5:1–2 says, "Be ye therefore followers of God, as dear children; And walk in love, as Christ also hath loved us, and hath given himself for us an offering and a sacrifice to God for a sweet smelling savor." Would you want your children to follow your ways? Do you walk in a godly love? Or do you walk as the world walks? Remember this: your walk talks *louder* than your talk talks. Is your testimony to the world pleasing to God? Would you be ashamed to show your real self to the church you belong to? If not, repent now so your joy may be full.

Proverbs 23:12–14 says, "Withhold not correction from the child: for if thou beatest him with the rod, he shall not die. Thou shalt beat him with the rod, and shalt deliver his soul from hell." We, as parents, must correct our children that they may know the errors of their ways. We do this because we love them. Parents that love their child like they should does not enjoy spanking their child.

As a born-again Christian, we are sons of God. Therefore, as His children, He expects us to obey His Word. However, when we do not obey His Word, God has to chasten us so we will realize the errors of our ways. God wants to fellowship with us at all times, but we let some sin come into our lives and get between God and us. Remember, God does not fellowship with sin. God will chasten His children because He loves them. God does not chasten His children the same way. Proverbs 3:11–12 says, "My son, despise not the chastening of the Lord; neither be weary of his correction: For whom the Lord loveth he correcteth; even as a father the son in whom he delighteth."

Hebrews 12:7–11 says, "If ye endure chastening, God dealeth with you as with sons; for what son is he whom the father chasteneth not? But if ye be without chastisement, whereof all are partakers, then are ye bastards, and not sons. Furthermore we have had fathers of our flesh which corrected us, and we give them reference: shall we not much rather be in subjection unto the Father of spirits, and live? For they verily for a few days chastened us after their own pleasure; but he for our profit, that we might be partakers of his holiness. Now no chastening for the present seemeth to be joyous, but grievous: nevertheless afterward it yieldeth the peaceable fruit of righteousness unto them which are exercised hereby."

We want to point out that God's main object in chastening you is to help you become more like Jesus so that you may enjoy being a part of the things of God. There are so many Christians today that are missing out of the things of God, such as the joy of their salvation, the power that awaits us in Christ Jesus, the great truth revealed in the Word of God by the leadership of the Holy Spirit of God, the peace that passes all understanding, and the hope we have in His coming again.

Christian friend, let us look at Ephesians 4. Verses 1–7 of chapter 4 says, "I therefore, the prisoner of the Lord, beseech you that ye walk worthy of the vocation wherewith ye are called. With all lowliness and meekness, with longsuffering, forbearing one another in love; Endeavoring to keep the unity of the Spirit in the bond of peace. There is one body, and one Spirit, even as ye are called in one hope of your calling; One Lord, one faith, one baptism, One God and Father of all, who is above all, and through all, and in you all. But unto every one of us is given grace according to the measure of the gift of Christ."

Many truths are found in these seven verses. We will point out a few. Dearly beloved, whether you are a pastor, teacher, preacher, evangelist, singer, music director, treasurer, or visitation minister, please be caution to heed to verses 1–3. If you say you are called to be this or that in the work of God, then you must be sure that your walk in this vocation is with "all lowliness and meekness, with longsuffering, forbearing one another in love; Endeavoring to keep the unity of the Spirit in the bond of peace." As Christians, God expects us to keep the spirit of unity in our hearts, for we are one body in Christ Jesus. We as born-again Christians have the same one Spirit of God abiding in us. Therefore, when we do anything for God, we should have the same goal. That goal should be to glorify God in all that we do. We must remember that we have one Lord, one faith, and one baptism. Is Jesus the Lord of your life in all things? Are you like some that let Jesus be Lord at their convenience? We have one faith. We were given that faith by the Lord Jesus Christ. We must live out that faith. *You* must work out your own salvation.

In other words, you must learn what God expects of you in your life. First, you must learn the basics for all Christians, which includes you. Then you must be obedient to Him and perform these tasks. As you practice doing these, you will grow in the Lord. Thus, you will be able to walk with him and learn to know His perfect will for your life. Whatever you do, do them for the glory of God, and you will be blessed more than you can ever imagine. We must remember that we are of one baptism. We, upon our spiritual birth, are baptized into the family of God by the Holy Spirit.

There is but "one God and Father of all, who is above all, and through all, and in you all." You see, we have only one God and only one Father. Therefore, we should not worship anyone else and called no one else Father. Yet through His wonderful grace, He has come and abided in us by His Spirit.

In verse 7, we see that "every one of us is given grace according to the measure of the gift of Christ." Dearly beloved, do not try to be what someone else is. Be yourself in Christ Jesus as God has given you talents to serve Him. Be thankful for the abilities that you have. Exercise these talents for the glory of God, and He will increase your talent the more. Do not waste your life away wishing you were someone else. You are very special to God. You have a special gift. You must use that gift even though you think it not to be important. My friend, all things that God's children do are important to Him, for you must answer to God for everything you do, whether it good or bad.

Let's look at Ephesians 4:11–16:

> And he gave some, apostles; and some, prophets; and some, evangelists; and some, pastors and teachers; For perfecting of the saints, for the work of the ministry, for the edifying of the body

of Christ: Till we all come in the unity of the faith, and of the knowledge of the Son of God, unto a perfect man, unto the measure of the stature of the fullness of Christ: That we henceforth be no more children, tossed to and fro, and carried about with every wind of doctrine, by sleight of men, and cunning craftiness, whereby they lie in wait to deceive; But speaking the truth in love, may grow up into him in all things, which is the head even Christ: From whom the whole body fitly joined together and compacted by that which every joint supplieth, according to the affectual working in the measure of every part, maketh increase of the body unto the edifying of itself in love.

There are some things we must bring to your attention from these verses. As we see in verse 11, God did not make everyone the pastor. God has chosen you for a purpose and can work that purpose in your life if you allow Him to have control of it. If you know God is calling you for a particular work in His service, then you should, by faith, yield to His calling. Be not afraid; He will give you all the strength and abilities to do the job He has called you to do. Don't forget that your work is very, very important in the service of God. How you are blessed is determined by how you work in this service. Remember this: Your work may not always be pleasing to man. However, you must never lose sight of whom you are pleasing. You must strive to please God in all things so your treasures may be stored in heaven for you. Never forget that Satan will always try to get your mind off what God has called you to do. Satan will show you other jobs that may be more soothing for the worldly Christian. Please do not yield to Satan's devices, for you will surely lose the joy of your salvation, and you will not have that peace that passes all understanding.

In verse 12, we see why God has given us different callings. It is for the perfecting of the saints. The Word of God tells us that we are to be "ye therefore perfect, for He is perfect" (James 1:4; James 2:22; James 3:2; 1 Peter 5:10). The word *perfect* mean we are to become mature in the Lord. *You* cannot become mature in the Lord if He is second in your life. *You* must strive to keep working to that end: to become more perfect in the things of God. This is what is meant in the Word of God when it says, "Work out your own salvation with fear and trembling. For it is God which woketh in you both to will and to do of his good pleasure" (Philippians 2:12–13). Please note that your salvation is of the *grace* of God, *not* of *works* (Ephesians 2:8–10). However, because of your faith and love of God, you will do good works for Him.

In Ephesians 4:11–13, we see that we have different callings for the edifying of the body of Christ. We, as Christians, are to build up one another in the Lord. Philippians 2:14–18 says. "Do all things without murmurings and disputings: That ye may be blameless and harmless the sons of God, without rebuke, in the midst of a crooked and perverse nation, among whom ye shine as lights in the world; Holding forth the word of life; that I may rejoice in the day of Christ, that I have not run in vain, neither labored in vain. Yea, and if I be offered upon the sacrifice and service of your faith, I joy, and rejoice with you all. For the same cause also do ye joy, and rejoice with me."

Christians need to stop all the murmuring and disputing. Christians are to work in unity of the faith. This is another reason God gave us different callings.

Ephesians 4:13 tells us, "Till we all come in unity of the faith, and of the knowledge of the Son of God, unto a perfect man, unto the measure of the stature of the fullness of Christ:" Throughout the Word of God, we see that God stresses His children to work in unity to accomplish the goal He has set before us as a church. We are to work toward being in unity of the faith. Also, verse 13 tells us we are to come in the unity "of the knowledge of the Son of God the stature of the fullness of Christ." As you see, God wants us to work toward that goal of being more like Jesus. Remember, the word *Christian* means to be like Christ.

Why do you think God wants us to be like Christ? Ephesians 4:14–16 tells us why:

> That henceforth be no more children, tossed to and fro, and carried about with every wind of doctrine, by the sleight of men, and cunning craftiness, whereby they lie in wait to deceive; But speaking the truth in love, may grow up into him all things, which is the head, even Christ: From whom the whole body fitly joined together and compacted by that which every joint supplieth, according to the effectual working in the measure of every part, maketh increase of the body unto the edifying of itself in love.

Let us look at a few verses of Ephesians 5. Verse 8 says, "For ye were sometimes darkness, but now are ye light in the Lord: walk as children of light." Is the light of Jesus shining in your life? Is your light like an old oil lamp that has a smutty globe that keeps most of the light from being seen? If you continue in sin, your globe will be so black the world will see no light in your life.

Do you want that peace that passes all understanding? If you do, you must lay aside any weight that besets you. Verses 14–17 says, "Wherefore he saith, Awake thou that sleepest, and arise from the dead and Christ shall give thee light. See then that ye walk circumspectly, not as fools, but as wise, Redeeming the time, because the days are evil. Wherefore be ye not unwise, but understanding what the *will of the Lord is*." Are you a sleeping Christian? If you are lying around and not serving God, then you must *wake up*. There is no more time for sleeping Christians. Time is running short, and we must get to work. We must arise from the dead (sleep). In other words, we are to be revived if we expect to do the will of the Father. We are to walk not as fools but wisely. We must redeem the time because the days are evil. The time God has given us must be used wisely. James 4:14–17 says, "Whereas ye know not what shall be on the tomorrow. For what is your life? It is even a vapor, that appareth for a little time, and then vanisheth away. For that ye ought to say, If the Lord will, we shall live, and do this, or that. But now ye rejoice in your boastings: all such rejoicing is evil. Therefore to him that knoweth to do good, and doeth it not, to him it is sin."

When traveling on the highways, you see a yield sign. This sign means you must slow down and look with caution before getting on the road. Beloved, if you just speed up and jump out on the road without yielding, you may come to an early grave. My friend, if you do not yield to the Holy Spirit of God, you may come to an early grave so your soul may be saved. (1 Corinthians 5:1–3).

My beloved, take a good look at yourself. What do you see? Are you happy? Are you pleased with what you are doing for God? My prayer is that you will live for Jesus so others will come to know him as Lord and Savior. As an obedient child of God, you will truly be blessed. Your treasures will be stored in heaven for you if your works are done for the glory of God. Always lift up Jesus in your life so all men will come to know Him (John 12:32). Jesus came that we might have life and have it abundance (John 10:10).

As you grow in the Lord, you will enjoy the walk with God. You will see that Satan is easier to overcome with the Lord. You will become stronger and be able to resist the devil (James 4:7). You will have strength to stay away from the appearance of evil, for you will see evil through the eyes of Jesus (1 Thessalonians 5:22).

In closing, my dearly beloved, I pray that you and I both can live as God would have us live, giving Him glory in all things so that we will have the peace that passes all understanding.

Christian friend, as Paul wrote to the church at Rome, "I beseech you therefore brethren, by the mercies of God, that ye present your bodies as living sacrifice, holy acceptable unto God, which is your reasonable service. And be not conformed to this world: but be ye transformed by the renewing of your mind, that ye may prove what is that good, and acceptable, and perfect, will of God" (Romans 12:1–2).

Dearly beloved, you must yield to the Holy Spirit at all times, or you will get on the wrong road of life, which leads to destruction. If you let God be your pilot, then your flight in this world will be more peaceful and rewarding. May you have peace with God all the days of your life.

Grace be unto you in the name of our Lord and Savior, Jesus Christ.

Ambassador of Truth,

Rev. Roger D. Cole

Ambassador of Truth Ministries

Mind? Heart? Salvation!

The people of today are a very troubled people as a whole. There is so much pressure from all directions. It may be family trouble. It may be political problems. It may be problems with friends. It may be job problems. It may be financial problems. My friend, usually the root of most problems come from self. If one does as most of the world does—looking out for number one first—life can and will be most miserable. The material things of this world will pass away. The honor and prestige will fade away. If these earthly pleasures and desires are first in your life, you are headed for very sad end. Jesus said, "But seek ye first the kingdom of God, and his righteousness? and all these things shall be added unto you" (Matthew 6: 33). Jesus is telling all people to seek first the kingdom of God and all His righteousness, then He will provide all our needs.

What is the kingdom of God? Matthew 3:1–2 says, "In those days came John the Baptist preaching in the wilderness of Judea, And saying, *Repent ye*: for the *Kingdom of Heaven* is at hand." Matthew 4: 17 says, "From that time Jesus began to preach, and to say, '*Repent*: for the *Kingdom of Heaven* is at hand.'" What were John the Baptist and Jesus saying? John the Baptist was preparing the way for the Lord (Matthew 3:3). He was letting people, the Jews, know that the Lamb of God, who takes away the sins of the world, was on the scene. Jesus Christ was saying the same thing. What kingdom were they talking about? What is this kingdom? This kingdom is the spiritual realm over which Jesus reigns as Lord and King.

You may ask, "How does a person become a part of Jesus's kingdom?" First, we must understand why Jesus had to come and die the sin death for you and me on the cruel cross of Calvary. God created Adam without sin. However, God created Adam with a will. Adam had the choice whether to obey God and live forever or disobey God and die. Adam chose to yield to the temptation of Satan, and he died spiritually. However, through God's infinite mercy, God chose to cover Adam's sin; by shedding the blood of animals, God covered Adam and Eve's nakedness (Genesis 3:21). The shedding of the blood of animals was used only so that sin could be covered. Note: The shedding of the blood of animals did not, and will not, take away sin. Thus, since Adam sinned, all humanity are born sinners. Because of Adam's sin, all humanity must die a fleshly death. Romans 5:12 says, "Wherefore, as by one man sin entered into the world, and death by sin; and so death passed upon all men for that all have sinned."

Throughout the old testament, you will find that God required certain sacrifices to be made and in a certain way and at a certain time. All these sacrifices were necessary to please God so that He would accept them as a covering of their sins. These sacrifices were a picture of the supreme sacrifice, the sacrifice of the Lamb of God for the sins of the world. The blood of animals could not take away the sins of the world; but the blood of Jesus, the Lamb of God, was the *only* one that could cleanse us from all unrighteousness. We want you to understand that there is no need for any other type of sacrifices to be made for your sins or mine. You must accept the Word of God as it is. Jesus's shedding His precious, pure blood on the cross was the *supreme sacrifice* for all the sins of the world (John 3:16).

What must you do to be a part of Jesus's kingdom? Let's explain what salvation is. All humanity is born with an eternal soul. Which means, the soul of man will exist forever, either in hell or heaven. Which place your soul goes? Only you can be sure of that. No one else can answer to God for you. You will answer to God for yourself (Romans 14:10–12). The priest or preacher or friend cannot answer to God for your soul. This is the most important matter that you will ever consider in your lifetime. Please consider this matter very seriously. The people of the Old Testament made the sacrifices as God commanded, for it was the law of God. However, since Jesus came, we are no longer under the law. We are under grace, which means unearned favor with God. Man must realize that he cannot earn his way to heaven. Because of the sin of Adam, death came upon all men. But through God's Son, and by His grace, we can have eternal life (Romans 5:21). *Salvation* of the soul is the deliverance of the soul from bondage of sin and the consequences of sin. In other words, salvation is the saving of a person's soul from eternal punishment and the admission of this soul into Jesus's spiritual kingdom (the family of God).

Now one may ask, "How does a person save their soul?" Many people will tell you this or that in order for you to save your soul. Caution: Do *not* believe this type of talk. *Only Jesus* can save the soul of man. You cannot save your own soul by doing this or that. If a person could get to heaven by their works, there would be no need of Jesus dying on the cross. You must come to God through Jesus Christ, God's way, or you will miss heaven. Man is so easily confused on the issue of salvation. It need not be so, for God is not the author of confusion (1 Corinthians 14:33). God, by His mercy and grace, has made salvation plain and clear.

Jesus said in John 14:6, "I am the way, the truth, and the life: no man cometh unto the Father, but by me." There is much said in these words of our Lord. As you see, if you want to go be with the Father in heaven, you must go through Jesus Christ, and Him alone. If you want to pray to the Heavenly Father, you must go through Jesus. As you must note: If you want to communicate with God for yourself or for anyone else, you can only achieve this through Jesus Christ. All other communication is of no effect. In order to please God, we must do as He says in His Word.

Man-made rules and regulations have caused many people to have a false security for their soul. If man is to please God, he must be willing to put traditions aside and turn to God, by grace, through the faith of our Lord Jesus Christ. Ephesians 2:1–10 explains what a person is before Salvation and how a person is saved and what a person should do after salvation. Verse 1 says, "And you hath he quickened, *who were dead in trespasses and sins*." Before salvation, our soul was *doomed* for hell because of sin. Verses 8 and 9 says, "For by grace are ye saved through faith; and that not of yourselves: *it is the gift of God*: Not of works, lest any man should boast." These verses explain how we are saved and how we cannot be saved. We cannot earn salvation. However, after salvation, we are to do *good* works. Verse 10 says, "For we are his workmanship, created in Christ Jesus unto good works."

Caution: Even though we are under Grace, we can only be saved in God's way. Remember, Jesus said in John 14:6, "I am *the Way, the Truth and the Life*: no man cometh unto the Father, but by me." Acts 4:12 says, "Neither is there salvation in any other: for there is none other name under heaven given among men, whereby we must be saved." Acts 4:5–11 explains the name referred to in verse 12, which is Jesus Christ of Nazareth. You may ask, "When can a person get saved?" Remember this: salvation is a gift of God. Thus, He will, through His Spirit, call a person unto salvation by His Word. What does this mean? Studying the first chapter of John, you will find that Jesus Christ is the Living Word of God. Always keep that in mind while studying God's Word. Acts 10:17 says, "So then faith cometh by hearing, and hearing by the Word of God." One must hear the Word of God, either from another individual or by the person of the Holy Spirit of God as one reads the Word of God. Whether man speaks the Word of God to you or you read the Word of God yourself, the Holy Spirit of God will move in your heart and convict you of your sin. The Holy Spirit will let you know, through the Word of God, that you were born a sinner because of Adam; and you must repent your sin and ask God, by His *grace*, through faith in Jesus Christ to save your soul. Caution: You must yield to the Holy Spirit, for you may not have another opportunity in your life to be saved. Second Corinthians 6:2 states, "Behold, now is the accepted time; behold, now is the day of Salvation." What does *repent* mean? *Repent* means to have a *change of heart*. In other words, you are saying to God, "I am sorry I sinned against You, God, and I will, by your grace, not continue in sin. Thus, I will not serve sin but serve You, God, with all my heart. I will not do what is displeasing in Your sight."

Because of Adam, all men are born with a sinful nature. Therefore, it's man's nature to want to sin. This is why, repentance toward God is part of the salvation plan of God. Where there is no true repentance toward God, there cannot be salvation of the soul. Repentance of a contrite heart toward God, and faith in Jesus Christ, will bring salvation of the soul. This is what is called the new birth (born again). Jesus explains this in the book of John chapter 3.

The heart of man (spiritually) is the innermost part of an individual. It could be said that the innermost part of an individual is one's soul. All men are born with a soul (a spirit). Given by God as part of this soul is a conscience, which is the moral sense of an individual.

In Matthew 22:37, Jesus said, "Thou shalt love the Lord thy God with all *thy heart*, and with all *thy soul*, and with all *thy mind*." *Soul* used in this verse, in the Greek, can be used as follows: referring to animals, *soul* means "life of the animal"; referring to plants, *soul* means "vitality or life"; and referring to mankind, *soul* means "heart, mind, life, and soul." The Greek word for *soul* is *psuche* (psoo-khay'). The Greek word for *heart* is *kardia* (kar-dee'ah), which means "the thoughts or feelings of the mind; also the center of one's thoughts or feelings." The Greek word for *mind* is *diavoia* (dee-an'oy-ah), which means "deepest thought, imagination, or understanding."

We must understand that God is a trinity. This means that the Godhead consists of three persons in one. Our God consists of the person of the Heavenly Father, the person of the only begotten Son, and the person of the Holy Spirit.

We hope this information will help you understand what God meant when He said in Genesis 1:26, "And God said, Let *us* make man in *our* image, after *our* likeness." When God used the words *us* and *our* in this verse, He was speaking of the Trinity of God, the Heavenly Father, Jesus Christ (God's only begotten Son), and the Holy Spirit. Thus, we must conclude that Jesus Christ was in existence before the beginning of time. Therefore, we see that there is no mention of God having a *mother*. He, God, was in existence before creation.

You may ask, "Where did God come from?" This is a normal question for you to ask. In Deuteronomy 29:29 God says, "The secret things belong the Lord our God; but those things which are revealed belong unto us and to our children for ever, that we may do all the words of this law." All of God's Word can be referred to as God's law. Some questions in life will not be answered until we get to heaven. However, God has given His Word unto us so that we may know how we ought to live and what we must do to inherit everlasting life. A lost person must repent and receive Jesus as Lord and Savior, through faith, in order to have everlasting life. A saved person (born again) must live by faith if they are to receive the joy of their salvation. Romans 1:17 says, "As it is written, The just shall live by faith."

For the heart of man to receive any communication with self, man, or God, he must receive it through his mind. The mind lets us know what our eyes see, what our ears hear, and all the other natural senses God has given us. The mind is the doorway to the heart of man. However, everything that goes through the mind does not, and should not, always be received into the heart. Man can open his heart only from the inside. Whatever he receives into his heart, he opens the door and allows it to come in. As you see, when Jesus comes and knocks at your heart's door, through the Holy Spirit of God, only you can open that door and let Jesus in. Jesus will come and abide in you, through the Holy Spirit of God, if you allow Him to do so. Jesus will not force you to receive Him. Jesus told His disciples to shake the dust off their feet and go somewhere else if someone would not hearken to the things of God (Mark 10:14).

Whatever you allow the most to go through your mind will be the thing that will influence your heart the most. God wants all men to repent and accept Jesus Christ as Lord and Savior. The gift of eternal life is for *all* men to receive. However, not *all* men will receive eternal life. Those that will reject salvation, God's way, will spend eternity in hell. God gives man the choice: heaven or hell for eternity.

Should man choose salvation, God's way, he then will be a new person. Second Corinthians 5:17 says, "Therefore, if any man be in Christ, he is a *new creature*: *old things* are passed away; behold, *all things* are become new." You, upon your new birth (spiritual), then become a member of the family of God. You are now a son of God (John 1:12). Now as a child of God, you are expected to be obedient to His Word. In John 14:15, Jesus said, "If ye love me, keep my commandments." In John 15:10 Jesus said, "If ye keep my commandments, ye shall abide in my love; even as I have kept my Father's commandments, and abide in His love."

Jesus is telling us that if we love Him, we are to follow His instructions completely or exactly as He said. What are His instructions? In His Word are all instruction given to us to live thereby.

What about the Ten Commandments given by God? The Ten Commandments were given so one could identify what is sin against God. The Ten Commandments are of the law of God. Thus, transgression of the law is sin (1 John 3: 4). Jesus said in Matthew 5:17, "Think not that I am come to destroy the law, or the prophets: I am not come to destroy, but to fulfill." The law and the prophets is the Old Testament. Jesus coming and dying on the cross is a fulfilling of Old Testament prophecy.

In Matthew 22:34–36, the Pharisees questioned Jesus. They asked Jesus, "What is the great commandment in the Law?" Jesus replied, in verses 37–40, "Thou shalt love the Lord thy God with all *thy heart*, and with all *thy soul*, and with all *thy mind*. This is the first and great commandment. And the second is like unto it, Thou shalt love thy neighbor as thyself. On these two commandments hang all the law and the prophets." Consequently, if a man keeps these two commandments, he will be pleasing to God. A child of God will do his best to obey his Heavenly Father in all things. However, should God's child disobey Him, God will chasten this child. At the moment of salvation (the new birth), the Holy Spirit of God comes and abides in you. Since He, the Holy Spirit, is God, He will let you know in your heart when you have sinned. Paul, writing to the Hebrews, who claimed to be believers, wrote these words in chapter 12:7–8:

> If ye endure chastening, God dealeth with you as with sons; for what son is he whom the father chasteneh not? But if ye be without chastisement, whereof all are partakers, then are ye bastards, and not sons.

As you can see, if you are not chastised when you sin, then you must not be a son of God (born again). If *you* are truly born again, you will know it in *your heart*. If you are saved and know it, your life will show it as pleasing God. Remember, James 2:10 says, "For whosoever shall keep the whole law, and yet offend in one point, he is guilty of all."

Since we as Christians have two natures, we will have a constant warfare between them. One nature, the flesh, will struggle against our new nature, the Spirit of God. If we yield to the flesh, we will sin. When a child of God sins, the Holy Spirit will convict him of this sin. Then we are to repent immediately (1 John 1 and 2). This will allow us to fellowship with our Heavenly Father, for God does not fellowship with sin. We must die to the flesh daily so that we may live for Christ daily.

My friend, are you one who *professes* Christ Jesus as Lord and Savior? Or are you one who *possesses* Christ Jesus in your heart? If you have been born again, you will know. And if you know you are saved, your life will show it. The evidence of salvation is true obedience to the Word of God. If Jesus lives within you, then you are the light of the world. The world must see Jesus in your life. Believing, in itself, is not enough. James 2:19–20 says, "Thou believest that there is one God; thou doest well: the devils also believe, and tremble. But wilt thou know, O vain man, that faith without works is dead." Ephesians 2:8–10 says, "For by Grace are ye saved through faith, and that not of yourselves: it is the gift of God. Not of works, lest any man should boast. For we are his workmanship, created in Christ Jesus unto good works, which God hath before ordained that we should walk in them." You are a new creature in Christ Jesus. Therefore, you should do what is pleasing to God and not what is pleasing to the flesh (2 Corinthians 5:17) Romans 12:1–2 says, "I beseech you therefore, brethren, by the mercies of God, that ye present your bodies a living sacrifice, holy, acceptable unto God, which is your reasonable service. And be not conformed to this world but be ye transformed by the renewing of your mind, that ye may prove what is that good, and acceptable, and perfect, will of God."

"Whether therefore ye eat, or drink, or whatsoever ye do, do all to the glory of God" (1 Corinthians 10:31). Is pleasing God first in your life? Are other people second in your life? Are you placing yourself third in your life? What you put first in your life is your God.

When an individual comes to the point where he or she knows in their heart that they are saved from eternal damnation and know that they have eternal life and know for sure that they are going to heaven, then they can truly say that they have a *heart of salvation*. A heart of salvation will produce a faithful witness for Christ. Thus, one will be pleasing to God rather than man. Otherwise, they may have professed but do not possess Jesus Christ in their heart. A profession of Jesus is only a *mind salvation*, which will only help you in the eye of man. This will not help the destination of your soul. Are you sure of your salvation? Have you been obedient to God's Word in baptism after your conversion (born again) (Romans 6:1–9)? You will never have the joy of His salvation if you cannot show your obedience to your Lord and Savior in the first command after salvation. Read Matthew 28:19–20, Acts 2:41, Matthew 3:13, and Acts 8:12. Remember this: James 4:17 says, "Therefore to him that knoweth to do good, and doeth it not, to him it is sin."

May the Holy Spirit of God guide you in the truth of God's Word so that you may know the destination of your soul before you die. First John 5:13 says, "These things have I written unto you that believe on the name of the Son of God; that ye may know that ye have eternal life, and that ye may believe on the name of the Son of God."

May the world see Jesus in all that you do, for His honor and glory. It is my prayer that Jesus Christ will be lifted up in our lives so that others may come to know Him as Lord and Savior.

Bro. R. D. Cole

Ambassador of Truth Ministries

Living by Faith

This subject is one to be dealt with very carefully. Preachers have told us many examples of great men of faith in the Bible. Throughout the ages, there has been many great Christians of faith. It is a joy to read and tell about these people of faith. Yet we need to see what we must do to become a Christian who will live by Faith.

First, we must understand what is faith according to the Word of God. Hebrews 11:1 says, "Now faith is the substance of things hoped for, the evidence of things not seen." In our little finite mind, we have a hard time understanding what all this really means. We must understand that God is the potter and we are the clay. We, in ourselves, cannot have the faith. Let me explain.

Galatians 2:15–21 says, "We who are Jews by nature, and not sinners of the Gentiles, Knowing that a man is not justified by the works of the law, *but by the faith of Jesus Christ*. Even we have believed in Jesus Christ, that we might be justified *by the faith of Christ*, and not by the works of the law: for by the works of the law shall no flesh be justified. But if, while we seek to be justified by Christ, we ourselves also are found sinners, is therefore Christ the minister of sin? God forbid. For if I build again the things which I destroyed, I make myself a transgressor. For I through the law am dead to the law, that I might live unto God. I am crucified with Christ: nevertheless I live; yet not I, but Christ liveth in me: and the life which I now live in the flesh I live by the faith of the Son of God, who loved me, and gave himself for me. I do not frustrate the grace of God: For if righteousness come by the law, then Christ is dead in vain."

We need to understand that Jesus Christ is our Creator and our Savior. Any communication to our Heavenly Father must be done through Jesus Christ. To glorify God in our lives, we must put Jesus in the center of it (the head of our lives).

Looking at the above verses, you can see that our faith is of Jesus Christ. For we would be nothing without Him. We, as Christians, have missed out on the best God has for us so many times. We have lived defeated lives without the joy and peace that God wants us to have. We have limited the power of God in our lives. We, as Christians, want the blessings of God without being obedient to His Word and without yielding to the Holy Spirit of God. You may wonder when you can know if the Holy Spirit is speaking to your heart or if it is the flesh. You *cannot be led* by the Holy Spirit unless you are *fed* by the Holy Spirit. As you learn more about the Word of God and live what you learned, then you will be more sure of what is speaking to you, whether it be the flesh or the Holy Spirit.

As a Christian, a born again, we have Christ living in us through the Holy Spirit of God. Hence, the faith we have is bestowed in us by Jesus Christ through the Holy Spirit of God. As Paul said, "I am crucified with Christ: nevertheless I live; yet not I, but Christ liveth in me: and the life which I now live in the flesh I live by the faith of the Son of God, who loved me, and gave himself for me."

We should be as Paul and understand that we are not our own anymore, for we were bought with the price of the precious blood of Christ. Now if you allow Jesus to be not only your Savior but also your Lord and Master, then you will let Him have complete control of your life. This is what God wants you to do so that you will be blessed in your obedience. All Christians want the best for their lives. Yet most Christians want to live as they think is best and not what God knows is best. God's Word shows us, through the Holy Spirit, how we should live our Christian life as pleasing to Him. So many Christians are afraid of the unknown. Anyone can live by sight, but to please God and to be rewarded of God, we must live by *faith*. Hebrews 11:6 says, *"But without faith it is impossible to please Him:*

for he that cometh to God must believe that He is, and that *He is a rewarder of them that diligently seek Him.*"

Ask yourself, "Am I pleasing God? Am I living my life by sight, or am I living by faith?" You may think, "What does God want from me?" God wants all of you. He loved you enough to send His only begotten Son to die the sin death for you. Christ died so you may live. As a Christian, your rewards here on earth and at the judgment seat of Christ are determined by how you live for Him.

To begin living by faith, one must put *all* his or her trust (heart, soul, and mind) in the hands of God. Believe me, as a young Christian, this is not always easy to do. However, if you remember that we are His sheep and that sheep put their lives in the Shepherd's hands, then with a humble heart, you can learn to let your Good Shepherd control all your comings and goings in life. We must not allow Satan to put fear in our hearts about the unknown. Let us look at 2 Timothy 1:7–9. It says, "For God hath not given us the spirit of fear; but of power, and of love, and of a sound mind. Be not thou therefore ashamed of the testimony of our Lord, nor of me his prisoner: but be thou partaker of the afflictions of the gospel according to the power of God; Who hath saved us, and called us with a holy calling, not according to our works, but according to his own purpose and grace, which was given us in Christ Jesus before the world began." We should not fear anything in this world. However, because we still have the flesh, we cannot be in the spirit at all times. Thus, in the flesh, we will have fear come upon us. But as Christians, we should not let this fear abound in our lives. We must turn this fear over to the Lord and let His power, which lives in us, be manifested so we can have complete victory over Satan.

What then should we fear? Proverbs 9:10 says, "The fear of the Lord is the beginning of wisdom: and the knowledge of the Holy is understanding." Jesus said in Matthew 10:28, "And fear not them which kill the body, but are not able to kill the soul: but rather fear him which is able to destroy both soul and body in hell."

You may ask, "How can I come to the point in my life that I can live by faith?" Jesus said in Matthew 22:37–40, "Thou shalt love the Lord thy God with all thy heart, and with all thy soul, and with all thy mind. This is the first and great commandment. And the second is like unto it, Thou shalt love thy neighbor as thyself. On these two commandments hang all the law and the prophets." If you can do this, then you will have no problem living by faith.

Proverbs 3:1–10 says, "My son, forget not my law; but let thine heart keep my commandments: For length of days, and long life, and peace, shall they add to thee. Let not mercy and truth forsake thee: bind them about thy neck; write them upon the table of thine heart; So shalt thou find favor and good understanding; in the sight of God and man. Trust in the Lord with all thine heart; and lean not unto thine own understanding. In all thy ways acknowledge him, and he shall direct thy paths. Be not wise in thine own eyes: fear the Lord, and depart from evil. It shall be health to thy navel, and marrow to thy bones. Honor the Lord with thy substance, and with the first fruits of all thine increase: So shall thy barns be filled with plenty, and thy presses shall burst out with new wine." There are so many things said in these few verses. What must I do to add days to my life and have peace? Verse 1 tells us. How can I find favor and good understanding in the sight of God and man? Verse 3 tells us. How can I know God will direct my paths in life? Verses 5 and 6 tells us. What must I do to have good health? Verse 7 tells us. How can I be blessed with material things on earth? Verse 9 tells us. Jesus said in Matthew 6:33, "But seek ye first the kingdom of God, and his righteousness; and all these things shall be added unto you." Because of many trials and tribulations, Christians have lost the joy of His salvation. Some have allowed Satan to win many battles in their lives. Jesus said in John 16:33, "These things I have spoken unto you, that in me ye might have peace. In the world ye shall have tribulation: but be of good cheer; I have overcome the world."

You have read how you can achieve the joy of living by faith. What do you intend to do about it? Are you willing to die to self daily and love the Lord with all your heart, your soul, and your mind? How happy you are as a child of God depends on your obedience to His Word.

As you step out in faith, you will grow stronger and wiser in the things of God. You will be blessed spiritually as well as physically. All your needs will be met, and many other blessings will be added unto you. The joy of His salvation will be restored unto you. You will have the peace that passes all understanding. You will be able to stay away from the appearance of evil. You will have more power in your life to not yield to temptation. You will be more disciplined to be faithful in the study of the Word of God. You will find time to be of service to your Lord in your local New Testament church. You will allow the Holy Spirit of God lead you in all that you do so you may glorify God in all that you do.

Remember this: you *cannot* live by faith in your own strength. You must give all of yourself to Christ so He can give you the faith to live by faith.

May God richly bless you as you start living by faith.

Yours in Christ,

Bro. Roger D. Cole
Ambassador of Truth

Ambassador of Truth Ministry

Remedy for False Teaching

Dearly beloved, there are so many teachings going around today that do not measure up to the whole counsel of God. We must remember that God is not the author of confusion. His Word is truth and His Word is complete. No one is to add or take away from the Word of God.

So many false teachings come from an individual taking the scripture out of context and using it to prove their point. Scripture must be interpreted with scripture. God does not lie. Therefore, the Word of God will not contradict itself. Sometimes, for us to get the full meaning of a scripture, we may have to read many verses before and after this verse. Sometimes, it may take many chapters or even the whole book to get the full meaning intended.

There are many, many self-made prophets in the world today. Many are blinded to the truth of God's Word. Thus, as the Word of God says, "*The blind shall lead the blind.*" So many people get so involved in their religion that they have no room for the Holy Spirit of God to teach them.

God has an order for everything. There should be order in the Worship of God, in the service of God, and in the study of His Word. If the things of God are not in His order, souls will not be saved and Christians will not grow spiritually.

Second Timothy 2:15–16 says, "Study to show thyself approved unto God, a workman that needeth not to be ashamed, rightly dividing the word of truth. But shun profane and vain babblings: for they will increase unto more ungodliness."

First John 4:1 says, "Beloved, believe not every spirit, but try the spirits whether they are of God: because many false prophets are out into the world." First John 4: 6 says, "We are of God: he that knoweth God heareth us: he that is not of God heareth not us. Hereby know we the spirit of truth, and the spirit of error."

Many teachers want Christians to look to them for wisdom of the scriptures. They have their reward, which is men following them and taking their eyes off Jesus. This is not God's order. Many people fall for this, for they are too lazy to study the scriptures for themselves. If you are not willing to study the Word of God, you will never know the true will of God for your life.

God has an order for us to learn His Word. Of course, God uses Holy Spirit-filled teachers to teach new converts to make disciples out of them. However, the best teacher is the Holy Spirit of God, who lives in born-again individuals.

We must realize that true wisdom comes from God. We can see what Paul meant in 1 Corinthians chapters 1 and 2. The wisdom of this world is foolishness to God. First Corinthians 1:20–21 says, "Where is the wise? Where is the scribe? Where is the disputer of this world? Hath God made foolish the wisdom of this world? For after that in the wisdom of God the world by wisdom knew not God, it pleased God by the foolishness of preaching to save them that believe."

All of us would like to be wiser. One that is wise in the Lord will be a witness for Christ so that others may come to Jesus for salvation. Proverbs 11:30 says, "The fruit of the righteous is a tree of life; but he that winneth souls is wise." When you witness to a lost person and they receive Jesus as their Lord and Savior, then you can say that a soul has been won to Christ. As a born-again believer, you must first be a witness for Christ. As you study the Word of God and let the Holy Spirit of God teach you in all truth, then you can become a better soul-winner.

Paul said, in chapter 2 verse 5 of 1 Corinthians, "That your faith should not stand in the wisdom of men, but in the *power of*

God." In verses 7–8 Paul said, "But we speak the wisdom of God in a mystery, even the hidden wisdom, which God ordained before the world unto our glory: Which none of the princes of this world knew: for had they known it, they would not have crucified the Lord of glory."

Dearly beloved, if you truly love God with all your heart, you should get excited about verse 9. Verse 9 says, "But as it is written, Eye hath not seen, nor ear heard, neither have entered into the heart of man, the things which God hat prepared for them that love him." Jesus said, "If you love me, keep my commandments." Jesus also said in John 10:10, "The thief cometh not, but for to steal, and to kill, and to destroy? I am come that they might have life, and that they might have it more abundantly." If you want to have all that God has to give you (abundant life), then you must give your *all* to Him daily. As Paul said, we must die to self daily. You can do this if you allow the Holy Spirit of God control your life. He will guide you into the truth of God's Word. John 14:23–26 says, "If a man love me, he will keep my words: and my Father will love him, and we will come unto him, and make our abode with him. He that loveth me not keepeth not my sayings: and the word which ye hear is not mine, but the father's which sent me. These things have I spoken unto you, being yet present with you. *But the Comforter, which is the Holy Ghost, whom the Father will send in my name, he shall teach you all things, and bring all things to your remembrance, whatsoever I have said unto you.*"

When you study the Word of God, you must allow God to speak to you by His Spirit. You must understand that your relationship with Jesus is personal. Therefore, you should personally see to it that you learn all you can about Him so you can be more pleasing to the Father. If you truly love someone, you will want to learn all you can about that person so you will be more able to show love more freely.

We want to be able to know if a teaching is false or not. If we know the truth of God's Word, then we should know what is not truth. Henceforth, we must study faithfully the Word of God and let His Spirit teach us. First Corinthians 2:10–13 says, "But God hath revealed them unto us by his Spirit: for the Spirit searcheth all things, yea, the deep things of God. For what man knoweth the things of a man, save the spirit of man which is in Him? Even so the things of God knoweth no man, but the Spirit of God. Now we have received, not the spirit of the world, but the Spirit which is of God; that we might know the things that are freely given to us of God. Which things also we speak, not in the words which man's wisdom teacheth, but which the Holy Ghost teacheth; comparing spiritual things with spiritual." We see that the Holy Spirit of God is the best teacher.

First John 2:18–29 says this:

> Little children, it is the last time: and as ye have heard that antichrist shall come, even now are there many antichrists; whereby we know that it is the last time. They went out from us, but they were not of us; for if they had been of us, they would no doubt have continued with us: but they went out, that they might be made manifest that they were not all of us. But ye have an unction from the Holy One, and ye know all things. I have not written unto you because ye know not the truth, but because ye know it, and that no lie is of the truth. Who is a liar but he that denieth that Jesus is the Christ? He is antichrist, that denieth the Father and the Son. Whosoever denieth the Son, the same hath not the Father: but he that acknowledgeth the Son hath the Father also. Let that, therefore abide in you, which ye have heard from the beginning. If that which ye have heard from the beginning shall remain in you, ye also shall continue in the Son, and in the Father. And this is the promise that he hath promised us, even eternal life. These things have I written unto you concerning them that seduce you. But the anointing which ye have received of him [Christ] abideth in you, and ye need not that any man teach you: but as the same anointing

teacheth you of all things, and is truth, and is no lie, and even as it [anointing] hath taught you ye shall abide in him. And now, little children, abide in him; that, when he shall appear, we may have confidence, and not be ashamed before him at his coming. If ye know that he is righteous, ye know that every one that doeth righteousness is born of him.

Dearly beloved, read these scriptures: Matthew 7:15–23 and Acts 20:17–32. Beware of the wolves! Beware of these signs and wonders of today! Read 2 Corinthians 11:1–15. Paul warns Christians about those that teach another gospel. We see in verses 13–15 that these are false apostles, deceitful workers, and are of Satan. Verses 14–15 says, "And no marvel? for Satan himself is transformed into an angel of light. Therefore it is no great thing if his ministers also be transformed as the ministers of righteousness; whose end shall be according to their works."

Read Colossians 2:6–23. Verses 6–7 says, "As ye have therefore received Christ Jesus the Lord, so walk ye in him: Rooted and built up in him and stablished in the faith, as ye have been taught, abounding therein with thanksgiving." Verse 8 says, "Beware lest any man spoil you through philosophy and vain deceit, after the tradition of men, after the rudiments of the world, and not after Christ."

Second Timothy 4:1–4 says, "I charge thee therefore before God, and the Lord Jesus Christ, who shall judge the quick and the dead at his appearing and his kingdom; Preach the word? be instant in season, out of season? reprove, rebuke, exhort with all long-suffering and doctrine. For the time will come when they will not endure sound doctrine? but after their own lusts shall they heap to themselves teachers, having itching ears? And they shall turn away their ears from the truth, and shall be turned unto fables."

Dearly beloved, if you want the best that God has for your life, then you must give Him your best. That means your all—mind, body, and soul. You must focus your life around Jesus. You must seek the *perfect will of God* for your life. When you find His will and *do it*, then you can rejoice in Jesus. To find God's Will for your life, you must study His Word faithfully and in order. You must pray faithfully and on a regular basis.

Please remember this: Only when men find their joy in doing the will of God has the law of God been written in their hearts.

My friend, the remedy for false teaching is always *truth* (Jesus). You must learn about truth (by studying the Word of God faithfully) and live what you have learned. The more you learn about truth, the easier it will be for you to see what is not truth.

May God richly bless you as you follow Him into all truth.

Yours in Christ,

Rev. Roger D. Cole

Bro. Roger D. Cole

GROWING IN HOLINESS

Sanctification

Introduction

Sanctification: The *act* of making *holy*. In an evangelical sense, it is the act of God's grace by which the affections of men are purified or alienated from sin and the world and exalted to a supreme love of God. Second Thessalonians 2:13, "'God hath from the beginning chosen you to Salvation, through sanctification of the Spirit and belief of the truth."

Sanctification: The act of consecrating or of setting apart for a sacred purpose.

Sanctified: Made holy, consecrated, set apart for sacred services.

Sanctify: In a general sense, to *cleanse, purify,* or make holy; purge. Also to separate, set apart, or appoint to a holy sacred or religious use. Genesis 2:3 says, "And God blessed the seventh day, and sanctified it."

Read 1 Thessalonians 5:12–24. Verse 23 says, "Sanctify you wholly completely cleanse you and make you complete in Christ." Read 1 Thessalonians 3:11–13. Verse 13 says "To the end he may stablish your hearts unblamable in Holiness before God."

Second Thessalonians 2:13 tells us, "But we are bound to give thanks always to God for you, brethren beloved of the Lord, because God hath from the beginning chosen you to Salvation through Sanctification of the Spirit and belief of the Truth." In First Peter

1:2, Peter writes to the saved (elect), "Elect according to therefore knowledge of God the Father, through Sanctification of the Spirit unto obedience and sprinkling of the blood of Jesus Christ; grace unto you, and peace, be multiplied." The Holy Spirit *is* our sanctifier through the Word of God.

Read 1 Timothy 4:1–5 (set apart for use). Verse 5 tells us, "For it is *sanctified* by the *Word of God*." In John 17:16–21, Jesus is praying to the Father. Verse 17 says "*Sanctify* them through thy truth *thy word is truth*." Jesus had already chosen (called, *set them apart*). Now Jesus wants the Father to cleanse them (*to make holy*).

Read 1 Thessalonians 3:11–13 and 4:1–7. Chapter 3 verse 13 says, "To the end he may stablish your hearts unblamable in *holiness* before God even our Father, at the coming of our Lord Jesus Christ with all his saints." We are to live unto *holiness*. Chapter 4:7 states, "For God hath not called us unto uncleanness, but unto *holiness*."

Leviticus 11:44 tells us, "For I am the Lord your God; ye shall therefore *sanctify* yourselves, and ye shall be *holy, for I am holy*." Sanctify yourselves—separate yourselves from the world, even though you live in this world. Spiritually speaking, you are not of this world. Be holy; let the Holy Spirit of God cleanse you through His Word for the Master's use. Read 2 Timothy 2:19–21; verse 21 says, "If a man therefore *purge* himself from these, he shall be a Vessel unto honor, sanctified, and meet [fit] for the *Master's use, and prepared* unto every good work."

Purge—to cleanse thoroughly.

Sanctified—to make holy or consecrate.

Read Deuteronomy 7:1–11. In verses 1–5, we see God commanding His *chosen* people to be separated from the other people of the world. In verses 6–11, God tells His chosen people (Israel) why He chose them, just as God has chosen you and me to be His sons and daughters, because He loves you and me. God has brought you out of the bondage of sin as He also has brought Israel out of bondage of the Egyptians. Because of John 3:16, we can have eternal life through Jesus Christ, our Lord. God has chosen Israel and you and me to be a holy people. Read Exodus 19:1–6. God called Israel to be a special people, a treasure, and a *holy nation*.

Isaiah 43:15 says, "I am the Lord, your Holy one, the creator of Israel, your King." Verse 21 states, "This people have I formed for myself; they shall show forth my praise." Verse 7 says, "Even everyone that is called by my name; for I have created them for my glory." First Corinthians 10:31 says, "Whatsoever ye do, do all to the glory of God."

As we grow in holiness, we then are to *sanctify* our God and Savior. Isaiah 5:16 tells us, "but the Lord of Hosts shall be exalted in judgment, and God that is Holy shall be *sanctified* in righteousness."

Sanctified—to put in a sacred place, to give the highest honor, hallow (holy).

To *sanctify God*—to praise and celebrate Him as a holy being, to *acknowledge* and *honor* His holy majesty, and to *reverence* His character and laws.

Isaiah 8:13 says, "*Sanctify* the Lord of Hosts himself; and let *Him* be your fear, and let *Him* be your dread."

Be sure! If God's people (born-again Christians or God's chosen people, the nation of Israel) do not sanctify God (put God where He should be in their lives as an individual or a nation), God will sanctify Himself or His name.

Read Ezekiel 36:1–38. Verses 22–23 tells us, "Therefore say unto the house of Israel, Thus saith the Lord God; I do not this for your sakes, O house of Israel, but for mine holy name's sake, which ye have profaned among the heathen, whither ye went. And I will sanctify my great name, which was profaned among the heathen, which ye have profaned in the midst of them: and the heathen shall know that I am the lord, saith the Lord God, when I shall be sanctified in you before their eyes."

God will always have the last say, and He will be honored and get all the glory.

Sanctification

Many questions arise when this subject is addressed. We hope you will have a better understanding of it after you have read this lesson.

Many churches or religions use these words—*sanctify*, *sanctified*, and *sanctification*. However, very few go into much detail of the meaning of these words. As you study the Word of God, it is more helpful if you have a clearer meaning of some words, such as these, as you come across them.

Usually, when a teacher or preacher speaks about the word *sanctify*, the definition used is this: "to set apart." There is much more to the meaning of this word.

According to *Webster's Dictionary*, the word *sanctify* means:

1. (A) to make sacred or holy
   (B) set apart to a sacred purpose or to religious use

2. (A) to make free from sin
   (B) cleanse from moral corruption and pollution (purify)

Sanctified means:

1. made holy
2. made free of sin or free from the bondage of sin

Sanctification means:

1. an act of sanctifying or of being sanctified
2. an act or process of growth in God's grace by which men are set free from the bondage of sin and exalted to a supreme

love of God and service to His kingdom under the inspiration of the Holy Spirit
3. the state of thus being purified (holiness)

In the study of the Word of God, we find that number 3 means: "divine perfection." We see that the sanctification of a born-again believer is threefold, which are as follows:

1. Positional sanctification
2. Progressive sanctification
3. Perfect sanctification

I

Let us look at *positional sanctification*. This refers to *our standing* before God, not our character. God has separated us to Himself; we stand before Him as perfect as Christ (in a spiritual sense), who is Himself our sanctification. First Corinthians 1:1–3 says, "Paul, called to be an apostle of Jesus Christ through the will of God, and Sosthenes our brother, Unto the church of God which is at Corinth, to them that are *sanctified* in Christ Jesus, called to be saints, with all that in every place call upon the name of Jesus Christ our Lord, both theirs and ours; Grace be unto you, and peace, from God our Father, and from the Lord Jesus Christ."

We must remember, as we study any subject, we must stay on this particular subject. There is so much that can be said about any part of the Word of God. We must make note that Paul was writing to born-again believers at the church of Corinth. First Corinthians 1:20–31 says, "Where is the wise? Where is the scribe? Where is the disputer of the world? Hath not God made foolish the wisdom of this world? For after that in the wisdom of God the world by wisdom knew not God, it pleased God by the foolishness of preaching to save them that believe. For the Jews require a sign, and the Greeks seek after wisdom: But we preach Christ crucified, unto the Jews a stumbling block, and unto the Greeks foolishness; But unto them which are called, both Jews and Greeks, Christ the power of God, and the wisdom of God. Because the foolishness of God is wiser than men; and the weakness of God is stronger than men. For ye see your calling, brethren, how that not many wise men after the flesh, not many mighty, not many noble, are called: But God hath chosen the foolish things of the world to confound the wise; and God hath chosen the weak things of the world to confound the things which are mighty; And base things of the world, and things which are despised, hath God chosen, yea, and things which are not, to bring to nought things that are: That no flesh should glory in his presence. But of him are ye in Christ Jesus, who of God is made unto us wisdom, and righteousness, and *sanctification*, and redemption: That according as it is written, He that glorieth, let them glory in the Lord."

When is one sanctified? At the time of conversion. Upon the conversion of Apostle Paul, we see these words spoken by our Lord: "I am Jesus whom thou persecutest. But rise, and stand upon thy feet: for I have appeared unto thee for this purpose, to make thee a minister and a witness both of these things which thou hast seen, and of those things in the which I will appear unto thee; Delivering thee from the people, and from the Gentiles, unto whom now I send thee, To open their eyes, and to turn them from darkness to light, and from the power of Satan unto God, that they may receive forgiveness of sins, and inheritance among them *which are sanctified by faith that is in me*" (Acts 26:15–18).

First Corinthians 6:9–20 says, "Know ye not that the unrighteousness shall not inherit the kingdom of God? Be not deceived: neither fornicators, nor idolaters, nor adulterers, nor effeminate, nor abusers of themselves with mankind, Nor thieves, nor covetous, nor drunkards, nor revilers, nor extortioners, shall inherit the kingdom of God. And such *were* [past tense] some of you: but *ye are* (present) washed, *but ye are sanctified,* but *ye are justified* in the name of the Lord Jesus and by the Spirit of our God. All things are lawful unto me, but all things are not expedient: all things are lawful for me, but I will not be brought under the power of any. Meats for the belly, and the belly for meats: but God shall destroy both it and them. Now the body is not for fornication, but for the Lord; and the Lord for the body. And God hath both raised up the Lord, and will also raise up us by his own power. Know ye not that your bodies are the members of Christ? Shall I then take the members of Christ, and make them the members of a harlot? God forbid. What? Know ye not that he which is joined to a harlot is one body? For two saith he, shall be one flesh. But he that is joined unto the Lord is one spirit. Flee fornication. Every sin that a man doeth is without the body; but he that committeth fornication sinneth against his own body. What? Know ye not that your body is the temple of the Holy Ghost which is in you, which ye have of God, and ye are not your own? For ye are bought with a price: therefore, glorify God in your body, and in your spirit, which are God's."

There was much sin in the church at Corinth. You must understand that a church of the Lord is a group of baptized believers. Some of the born-again believers in the church at Corinth were engaging in fornication. Paul was rebuking them with the Word of God. This discussed Paul deeply. Thus, he reminded them of their *position in Christ Jesus*. Paul reminded them that their bodies *are* (present position) the members of Christ (verse 15). He also reminded them that their body *is* (present position) the temple of the Holy Ghost, which *is* (present position) in you.

You may wonder, *How can this be?* In our own wisdom and power, this cannot be. But *only* by Jesus Christ our Lord, *is this so*. Paul, writing to the Hebrew Christians, referred to the Old Covenant and what it failed to do. He explained very plainly how the first covenant was taken away so that the second covenant could be established (Hebrews 10). Hebrews 10:9–10 says, "Then said he, Lo, I come to do thy will, O God. He taketh away the first, that he may establish the second. By the which will we *are* [present position] *sanctified* through the offering of the body of Jesus Christ *once for all*."

After an individual has been convicted of his sin by the Holy Spirit of God and has repented of his sin and asked Jesus to come into his heart for salvation and to be Lord of his life, then—and only then—can one say he is in this *position of sanctification*.

You must understand that the present position of sanctification we are in is because of Christ Jesus our Lord, and nobody else.

II

Let's look at *progressive sanctification.* Progressive sanctification refers to the actual daily experience of separating yourself from sin to God.

When does this happen? This a continual process of growth (spiritually) from the time of conception (the new birth) until one's flesh dies. This is a continual cleansing of one's life so he can be conformed into the image of Christ. This is what God expects out of you and me. Romans 12:1–2 says, "I beseech you therefore, brethren, by the mercies of God, that ye present your bodies a living sacrifice, holy, acceptable unto God, which is your reasonable service. And be not conformed to this world: but be ye transformed by the renewing of your mind, that ye may prove what is that good, and acceptable, and perfect will of God."

Paul, writing to the Corinthian church, says in 2 Corinthians 6:14–7:1, "Be ye not unequally yoked together with unbelievers: for what fellowship hath righteousness with unrighteousness? And what communion hath light with darkness? And what concord hath Christ with Belial? Or what part hath he that believeth with an infidel? And what agreement hath the temple of God with idols? For *ye are the temple of the living God?* as God hath said, I will dwell in them, and walk in them; and I will be their God. And they shall be my people. Wherefore come out from among them, and be ye separate, saith the Lord, and touch not the unclean thing: and I will be a father unto you, and ye shall be my sons and daughters, saith the Lord Almighty. Having therefore these promises, dearly beloved, let us *cleanse* ourselves from all filthiness of the flesh and spirit, *perfecting holiness* [sanctification] in the fear of God."

We must remember that all people are part of His creation, but not all people are His children. John 1:12–13 says, "But as many as received him, to them gave he power *to become the sons of God,* even to them that believe on his name: Which were born, not of blood, nor of the *will of the flesh, nor of the will of man, but of God.*"

As you see, we (born-again believers) became a child of God at the moment of salvation. Thus, we become heirs and joint-heirs with

Christ Jesus. Romans 8:16–17 says, "The Spirit itself beareth witness with our spirit, that we are the children of God: And if children, then heirs; heirs of God, and joint-heirs with Christ; if so be that we suffer with him [in this present world], that we may be also glorified together [this is at the moment of the rapture of the church; complete or perfect sanctification]."

Since we are part of the family of God, we should always be willing to please our Heavenly Father in all things. The short time given us here should be dedicated to the cause of Christ. We should be as Christ and seek out souls for His kingdom. We must learn all that we can about our Lord and Savior so that we may know how we should walk in this present world. We must be faithful in all things pertaining to God, especially the study of His Word.

The Word of God is the *cleansing agent* to be used to make this vessel a *vessel of honor* glorifying God in all things. Until this flesh is done away with, we are to keep it as clean as possible so that it can be used for the glory of God. It is just like a lamp globe; it must be cleaned daily, so the brightest light (Jesus) can be seen in our lives. Second Timothy 2: 21 says, "If a man therefore purge himself from these, he shall be a vessel unto honor, *sanctified*, and meet for the master's use, and prepared unto every good work."

Ephesians 5:25–26 says, "Husbands, love your wives, even as Christ also loved the Church, and gave himself for it; That he might *sanctify and cleanse it with the washing of water by the Word.*" As Jesus was praying to the Heavenly Father, He said, "*Sanctify them through thy truth; the Word is truth*" (John 17:17).

III

Let's look at the third phase of sanctification: *perfect sanctification*, which means the final and complete work of Christ at His coming (rapture) when He will remove us from all contact with sin. Ephesians 5:27 will come to past: "That He might present it [the church], to Himself a glorious church, not having spot, or wrinkle, or any such thing; but that it should be holy and without blemish."

Jesus will present His bride (the church) to Himself a glorious church, for the church (all born-again believers) has been cleansed by the Living Word, which is Jesus Himself. Surely, you must see that all things are *for* Him and *by* Him.

When Christ comes (the rapture) to get His church, each member of His church will be changed from corruptible to incorruptible in the twinkling of an eye. In other words, our body will be change into a glorified body, one without blood, one like our Lord and Savior.

We must share some scriptures with you. In 1 Corinthians 15, Paul was talking to the believers at Corinth about the resurrection of Christ and what it meant for all us believers in Christ. Let's look at verses 42–58. These verses say,

> So also is the resurrection of the dead. It is sown in corruption; it is raised in incorruption: It is sown in dishonor; it is raised in glory: it is sown in weakness; it is raised in power; It is sown a natural body; it is raised a spiritual body. There is a natural body, and there is a spiritual body. And so it is written, The first man Adam was made a living soul; the last Adam [Christ] was made a quickening spirit. Howbeit that was not first which is spiritual, but that which is natural; and afterward that which is spiritual. The first man is of the earth, earthy: the second man is the Lord from heaven. As is the earthy, such are they also that are earthy: and as is the heavenly, such are they also that are heavenly. And as we have borne the image of the earthy, we shall also bear the image of the heavenly. Now this I say, brethren, that flesh and blood cannot inherit the kingdom of God; neither doth corruption inherit incorruption. Behold, I show you a mystery; We shall not all sleep, but we shall all be change In a moment, in the twinkling of an eye, at the last

trump [this is the rapture]: for the trumpet shall sound, and the dead shall be raised incorruptible, and we shall be changed. For this corruptible must put on incorruption, and this mortal must put on immortality. So when this corruptible shall have put on incorruption, and this mortal shall have put on immortality, then shall be brought to pass the saying that is written, Death is swallowed up in victory. O death, where is thy sting? O grave, where is thy victory? The sting of death is sin; and the strength of sin is the law. But thanks be to God, which giveth us the victory through our Lord Jesus Christ [grace]. Therefore, my beloved brethren, be ye steadfast, unmovable, always abounding in the work of the Lord, forasmuch as ye know that your labor is not in vain in the Lord."

As we have indicated, *perfect sanctification* is done at the coming of our Lord (rapture). We must emphasize that, though the word *rapture* is not in the Word of God, the meaning of the word is. Thus, the word is used often in referring to the *Second Coming* of our Lord. The word *rapture* comes from the Latin word *rapere*. It means "to be caught up or caught away." Rapture also implies to being caught up in a state of happiness. The word is often used to describe the happiness of a bride on her wedding day. In the scriptures, Jesus Christ is referred to as the bridegroom, and the church as His espoused; and the Bible teaches that one day, Christ will return and catch up, or *rapture* His bride.

First Thessalonians 4:16–17 says, "For the Lord himself shall descend from heaven with a shout, with the voice of the archangel, and with the trump of God: and the dead in Christ shall rise first: Then we which are alive and remain shall be caught up together with them in the clouds, to meet the Lord in the air: and so shall we ever be with the Lord."

Philippians 3:17–21 says, "Brethren, be followers together of me, and mark them which walk so as ye have us for an example. For many walk, of whom I have told you often, and now tell you even weeping, that they are the enemies of the cross of Christ: Whose end is destruction, whose God is their belly, and whose glory is in their shame, who mind earthly things. For our conversation is in heaven from whence also we look for the Savior, the Lord Jesus Christ: Who shall change our vile body, that it may be fashioned like unto his glorious body, according to the working whereby he is able even to subdue all things unto himself."

First Thessalonians 3:11–13 says, "Now God himself and our Father, and our Lord Jesus Christ, direct our way unto you. And the Lord make you to increase and abound in love one toward another, and toward all men, even as we do toward you: To the end he may stablish your hearts unblamable in holiness before God even our Father, at the coming of our Lord Jesus Christ with all his saints."

First Thessalonians 5:12–28 says, "And we beseech you, brethren, to know them which labor among you, and are over you in the Lord, and admonish you; And to esteem them very highly in love for their work's sake. And be at peace among yourselves. Now we exhort you, brethren, warn them that are unruly, comfort the feebleminded, support the weak, be patient toward all men. See that none render evil for evil unto any man; but ever follow that which is good, both among yourselves, and to all men. Rejoice evermore. Pray without ceasing. In everything give thanks: for this is the will of God in Christ Jesus concerning you. Quench not the Spirit. Despise not prophesyings. Prove all things; hold fast that which is good. Abstain from all appearance of evil. And the very God of peace *sanctify* you wholly; and I pray God your whole spirit and soul and body be preserved [kept] blameless *unto the coming of our Lord Jesus Christ*. Faithful is he that calleth you, who also will do it. Brethren, pray for us. Greet all the brethren with a holy kiss. I charge you by the Lord that this epistle be read unto all the holy brethren. The grace of our Lord Jesus Christ be with you. Amen."

First John 3:1–2 says, "Behold, what manner of love the Father hath bestowed upon us, that we should be called the sons of God:

therefore, the world knoweth us not, because it knew him not. Beloved, now are we the sons of God, and it doth not yet appear what we shall be: but we know that, when he shall appear, *we shall be Like him* [perfect sanctification]; for we shall see him as he is."

Summary

The center of all things should be Christ. John 14:6 says, "Jesus saith unto him, I am the way, the truth, and the life: no man cometh unto the Father, but by me." We also must remember that an individual cannot come to the Father at his or her convenience. He must come when the Father draws him unto Himself (John 6:44). Romans 10:17 says, "So then faith cometh by hearing, and hearing by the word of God." This is done by the Holy Spirit of God when the Word of God is revealed unto them. Upon conviction of the Holy Spirit of God, an individual must repent of his sin and ask Jesus to not only save his soul but allow Jesus to become Lord of his life. In other words, he must die to self so that he may live in Jesus. At that moment, the Holy Spirit of God comes and abides within the believer. This is the *new birth* (spiritual birth or born again). From that moment, you are sanctified in Jesus Christ. This is the position you are in Jesus. This is what we call *positional sanctification*. At this moment, the new birth, you also begin to enter into what we call *progressive sanctification* (the beginning of your spiritual growth process).

You must understand that you have died to self, but you have not done away with the fleshly nature. You have added a *new nature*—the God nature. Upon true repentance, a believer will be a new person. Second Corinthians 5:17 says, "Therefore if any man be in Christ, he is a new creature: old things are passed away; behold, all things are become new." Your wants have changed. Your greatest desire is to *love* the Lord God with *all* your heart, body and soul, which is the first commandment. Remember this: God does not fellowship with sin. That is why He will let us know, by His Spirit, through His Word, what sin is in our lives.

There are many things a babe in Christ must learn. Like a new baby, someone that is mature in the Lord should be there for spiritual guidance to help this babe in Christ grow in a way that is pleasing to God. As one grows, he will learn to seek wise counsel and not believe just any wind of doctrine.

Dearly beloved, please remember that it is not what you do for God that will bring you closer to Him, but it is you getting closer to God that will cause you to do more for Him. You cannot work your way into a relationship with God. You must let His Spirit, which lives in you, guide you into this closer relationship. As you grow closer to the Lord, you will become stronger so that you may defeat all Satan throws your way. However, you must realize, as Paul, that as long as we have this fleshly body, we will be in a constant warfare; our old nature will be in conflict with the new, the God nature.

Paul, writing to the believers (saints), which are at Ephesus (Ephesians 1:1), says in chapter 6:10–20, "Finally, my brethren, be strong in the Lord, and in the power of his might. Put on the whole armor of God, that ye may be able to stand against the wiles of the devil. For we wrestle not against flesh and blood, but against principalities, against powers, against the rulers of the darkness of this world, against spiritual wickedness in high places. Wherefore take unto you the whole armor of God, that ye may be able to withstand in the evil day, and having done all, to stand. Stand therefore, having you loins girt about with truth, and having on the breastplate of righteousness; And your feet shod with the preparation of the gospel of peace; Above all, taking the shield of faith, wherewith ye shall be able to quench all the fiery darts of the wicked. And take the helmet of salvation, and the sword of the Spirit, which is the Word of God; Praying always with all prayer and supplication in the Spirit, and watching thereunto with all perseverance and supplication for all saints; And for me, that utterance may be given unto me, that I may open my mouth boldly, to make known the mystery of the gospel, For which I am an ambassador in bonds: that therein I may speak boldly, as I ought to speak."

As you see, we are soldiers for Christ. We are His, for we were bought with a price (His precious blood). Thus, we must prepare ourselves for a spiritual warfare. As you grow in the Lord, you will gain more confidence in your spiritual walk. You will have many tribulations while here on earth, yet you must be of good cheer, for our Lord has overcome the world. That is why we must realize that Jesus gave us not the spirit of fear, but *of power*. Henceforth, we can say that we can be more than conquerors in Christ Jesus.

Read Romans 8:28–39. Let's look at verses 28 and 37–39. Verse 28 says, "And we know that all things work together for good to them that love God, to them who are the *called* according to his purpose." Remember when the Holy Spirit convicted your sin and your need for salvation. This was when God called you unto Himself, as John 6:44 says. If you love God, then you will understand that all things that has happen in your Christian life is for your good and for His purpose.

Verses 37–39 says, "Nay, in all these things we are more than conquerors through him that loved us. For I am persuaded, that neither death, nor life, nor angels, nor principalities, nor powers, nor things present, nor things to come, Nor height, nor depth, nor any other creature, shall be able to separate us from the love of God, which is in Christ Jesus our Lord." If you have determined in your heart to think as Paul has said in verses 37–39, then you must be willing to serve God with all your heart.

Romans 12:1–2 says, "I beseech you therefore, brethren, by the mercies of God, that ye present your bodies a living sacrifice, holy acceptable unto God, which is your reasonable service. And be not conformed to this world: but be ye transformed by the renewing of your mind, they ye may prove what is that good, and acceptable, and perfect, will of God."

During your life as a Christian on earth, your mind will be renewed about many things as you are obedient to the Word by the leadership of the Holy Spirit in Christ Jesus. You need to look at yourself as a vessel to be used for the glory of God. You are the light of the world since Jesus lives in you. Like a globe, you must clean yourself from the inside so the world can see that light. You must let the Holy Spirit of God convict your heart of anything that may come between you and God, for God *does not* fellowship with sin.

Then like the globe on the lamp, more of the impurities are removed from your life and the world could see the light (Jesus) more clearly. Remember, this is done from within the heart, but the results will show on the outside. Don't forget, you cannot work yourself to God. You must let Him work in and through you, for He is the potter, and we are the clay. Let Him mold and shape you into a vessel of honor.

If you allow God to be first in all things and strive to do all things for His Glory, then you can truly say you have that peace that passes all understand. Thus, you can say "I understand what *progressive sanctification* is all about."

Perfect sanctification is the final and complete work of Christ at His Second Coming, when He will remove us from all contact with sin so He can present His bride (us—born-again believers) unto Himself, a glorious church without blemish.

We must understand that we cannot live above sin ("For all have sinned and come short of the Glory of God" [Romans 3:23]). However, when we are filled with the Spirit of God (in other words, when we have allowed the Holy Spirit of God to have full control of our body and soul), then we will not sin; for the Holy Spirit is God, and God does not fellowship with sin. As you mature in the Lord, your walk with Jesus will become purer. He said for us to be perfect (mature in the Lord), as He is perfect. We are to strive to be more like Christ in our Christian walk. The word *Christian* means to be Christlike. Read 1 John 1 and 2. You will see John writing to Christians and emphasizing the goodness of Christ and our weakness in self. John lets us know we are not sinless as a Christian, but we do have an advocate on the right hand of the Father: Jesus Christ. He also tells us how we should live as a Christian in order to fellowship with the Father.

Once a Christian realizes what they are and who they are in Christ, then one can really begin to grow in the Lord. We must realize we are nothing without Christ, but we can be all things in Christ. God created man. He knows the heart of man. That is why He emphasized so much in His Word the weakness of man. He said when we are made weak, He is strong. You see, when we are weak, we turn to Jesus for help. That is when He is lifted up in our lives. *He is strong for us.*

We, as Christians, have that blessed hope of Christ coming in the clouds to take us out (rapture) of this world and to ever be with Him (1 Thessalonians 4:13–18). This is the time of complete and perfect sanctification.

Oh, dearly beloved, we should rejoice, looking for His coming, and comfort one another with these words (1 Thessalonians 4:18).

Dearly beloved, please do not let anyone confuse you with every wind of doctrine. Let the Holy Spirit of God guide you into all truth (Jesus). He will not confuse you, for God is not the author of confusion. Be cautious about new doctrines. Study them for yourself. Don't be afraid to ask questions.

May the grace of God be with you as you serve Him with all your heart, body, and soul.

To God be the glory in all things.

Bro. Roger D. Cole
Ambassador of Truth

About the Author

Rev. Roger Cole was born a few months after World War II in Central Louisiana. He was blessed to live near a levee. On the other side of the levee was a bayou called Bayou Des Glaises as well as swamps. The bayou and the swamps were a major spot to get food for the family. The Lord always provided what was needed. There was no electricity and no running water. His dad built their two-room house for $150, and the chimney cost $50. His mom would cook on the fireplace, and they had an outside toilet—the old-fashioned type. His dad was raised Baptist. His mom was raised Catholic.

At eight years old, he moved to Leesville, Louisiana. His dad was a truck driver for a lumber company. The owner of the lumber company was the head deacon of a Baptist church. Roger Cole began going to church with the deacon. At ten years old, he realized he was lost, and the Holy Spirit moved on his heart that he should go to the altar and ask Jesus to come into his heart and save his soul.

It's been a long journey, yet with the Lord's help, Roger overcame the trials in life one day at a time. The heartaches and sorrows of losing two precious wives to cancer and the loss of one of his sons to a heart attack have helped him to be more dependent on his Lord for wisdom to help others as they go through similar heartaches and sorrows (2 Corinthians 1).

His present wife, whom the Lord has blessed him with for the last nine years, has lost two husbands to heart problems and has lost her only son to a heart attack.

His main goal in life as a minister of the gospel is to be the best husband he can be and, most of all, to share the love of God to as many people possible so that they may be born again and that they may grow with the Lord as they study the Word of God.

Roger surrendered to preach in 1976. He took a missionary trip in 1983 and spent one month in the Philippines. He supplied for thirty-one years, was a visitation minister for six years, pastored for six years, and was a song leader for seven years.

CPSIA information can be obtained
at www.ICGtesting.com
Printed in the USA
LVHW032342300621
691513LV00002B/138